Testbuch
ENGLISCH
7.–8. Klasse

W0191414

www.schuelerhilfe.de

© 2018 ZGS Bildungs-GmbH, Ludwig-Erhard-Str. 2, 45891 Gelsenkirchen

Herausgeber: ZGS Bildungs-GmbH, Gelsenkirchen
Redaktionsleitung: ZGS Bildungs-GmbH, Gelsenkirchen
Layout: Maria Mandelkow, zweiband.media, Berlin
technische Umsetzung: zweiband.media, Berlin
Lektorat/Korrektorat: ZGS Bildungs-GmbH, Gelsenkirchen
Umschlaggestaltung: Trapps Team für Kommunikation GmbH, Hamburg
Umschlagabbildung: ZGS Bildungs-GmbH, Gelsenkirchen

Liebe Schülerin, lieber Schüler!

„Übung macht den Meister.“

Du kennst dieses Sprichwort. Beim ersten Mal Lesen sagst du „ja, das stimmt".

Doch dann kommen dir Zweifel: Üben kostet doch Zeit, ist anstrengend, und eigentlich weiß ich doch Besseres mit meiner Zeit anzufangen. Ja, auch das mag stimmen. Doch mit einem kleinen Trick kann das Üben sogar Spaß machen. Der Trick besteht erstens darin, in kleinen Portionen zu üben, und zweitens, dieses regelmäßig zu tun.

In dem vorliegenden Testbuch haben deine Trainer diesen Trick eingebaut: Du findest pro Seite eine kleine Lernportion, die du bearbeitest – sehr überschaubar und frei nach dem Motto „In der Kürze liegt die Würze".

Für die richtigen Lösungswege kannst du dir Musteraufgaben auch online ansehen.

Suche dir einfach die für dich passendste Lernalternative aus – eine wirklich innovative Art des Lernens! Dabei sind die Tests überschaubar, vermitteln dir die Lerninhalte sehr anschaulich und motivieren dich zum Lernen.

Der wichtigste Vorteil ist, dass ein solches Lernen wenig Zeit beansprucht. Das Schülerhilfe-Testbuch eignet sich also ideal, mehrmals wöchentlich eine kleine Übungseinheit einzubauen. Du wirst sehen: Damit kommt Langeweile gar nicht erst auf, und du schaffst es ganz leicht mäßig, aber regelmäßig zu üben!

Wenn du zum Beispiel täglich nach den Hausaufgaben noch eine Seite aus dem Testbuch bearbeitest, ist das das ideale Zusatztraining, um deine Noten langfristig zu verbessern. Wichtig ist, dass du dich nicht überforderst! Ein Üben mit dem Testbuch nach dem Motto „mäßig, aber regelmäßig" frisst keine wertvolle Freizeit, und die Anstrengung hält sich auch in Grenzen. Denn Lernen soll schließlich Spaß machen!

Viel Spaß und Erfolg bei deinen Trainingseinheiten!

Prof. Dr. Ludwig Haag
Lehrstuhl für Schulpädagogik
Kulturwissenschaftliche Fakultät der Universität Bayreuth
Mitglied des Pädagogischen Beirats der Schülerhilfe Deutschland

Zur Arbeit mit diesem Buch

Dieses Testbuch ist die ideale **Übungsergänzung** zur **Lernhilfe** „Gute Noten mit der Schülerhilfe" Englisch Klasse 7/8.
Sie bietet dir über **250 Tests** im Buch & online zu genau deinen Englisch-Themen, die du gerade im Unterricht behandelst: hiermit kannst du dein Wissen festigen und dieses in zusätzlichen Übungen trainieren.

Dieses Übungsbuch ist eine Kombination aus Buch- und digitalen Lerninhalten, das ideal auf deine Schulinhalte abgestimmt ist.

Es bietet dir zusätzlich zur Lernhilfe:
- thematisch aufgebaute **Tests in 3 Schwierigkeitsstufen**
  Zeichenerklärung: ▉▉☐☐ = leicht, ▉▉▉☐ = mittel, ▉▉▉▉ = schwierig
- alle **Lösungen** zu allen Testaufgaben hinten im Anhang
- einen themenübergreifenden **Abschlusstest** am Ende des Buches
- viele **Musteraufgaben** online mit Erklärung des richtigen Lösungsweges

So arbeitest du am besten mit diesem Testbuch:

1. SCHRITT Beginne mit Test 1 des Testbuches und probiere alle Aufgaben selbstständig zu lösen.

2. SCHRITT Nachdem du den Test vollständig bearbeitet hast, bewerte nach den Lösungen im Anhang, wie viele Aufgaben du richtig gelöst hast und vergebe hierfür Punkte, die du in die Punktekästen auf jedem Testblatt eintragen kannst.

3. SCHRITT Hast du 80 % der Punkte eines Tests erreicht (Die genaue Anzahl der Punkte ist immer ganz unten auf jeder Testseite angegeben.), gehe weiter zum nächsten Test. Bei weniger erreichten Punkten wiederhole den Test noch einmal.

4. SCHRITT Bei Problemen mit den Aufgaben stehen dir zahlreiche Musteraufgaben zu vielen Aufgabentypen im Online-LernCenter zur Verfügung, die dir exemplarisch den richtigen Lösungsweg noch einmal erklären.

Wenn du alle Tests im Buch zu deinem Thema gelöst hast, findest du weitere **Übungsaufgaben, Lernvideos und Erklärungen** in digitaler Form im Online-Lerncenter der Schülerhilfe. Der **QR- und der Webcode** auf jeder Testseite führen dich direkt auf die richtige Seite im Online-Lerncenter.

Du hast hier 2 Möglichkeiten, so funktioniert es:

1. **Scanne den QR-Code,** den du auf deiner Testseite unten findest.
Du wirst dann direkt zu deinem Thema in das Online-Lerncenter geleitet. Hier kannst du dann zusätzliche Aufgabenblätter zum Üben herunterladen, dir Lernvideos ansehen oder Erklärungen zum Thema nachlesen.

2. Gehe auf die Seite **www.schuelerhilfe.de/gute-noten** und gib dann den **4-stelligen Webcode,** den du unten auf deiner Testseite findest, in das vorgesehene Eingabefeld ein. Du wirst dann im Online-Lerncenter direkt zu deinem Thema weitergeleitet.

oder:
www.schuelerhilfe.de
/gute-noten
CODE 5489

Inhaltsverzeichnis

Inhaltsverzeichnis

Die Zeiten – Das Present Perfect

Test 1   Present Perfect – simple form

Schwierigkeits-grad

A1   **Kreuze an, welche Sätze richtig im Present Perfect stehen.**   7

		richtig	falsch
a)	She speaks Dutch.	☐	☐
b)	Tom has been in his room.	☐	☐
c)	Paul have not forgotten his homework.	☐	☐
d)	Annie has kiss her boyfriend Oliver.	☐	☐
e)	They have bringing the tea.	☐	☐
f)	My dad has paid the bill.	☐	☐
g)	You have rent a car.	☐	☐

A2   **Bilde Sätze im *Present Perfect*.**   7

a) Thomas / not / *(to)* miss / the exam _____

b) We / *(to)* plant / some trees / in our / garden _____

c) We / *(to)* sell / our old car / to friends of the family _____

d) The train / *(to)* leave / the station _____

e) I / *(to)* spend / a lot of money _____

f) He / *(to)* read / four sides of the newspaper _____

g) You / *(to)* drive / much more slowly _____

oder:
www.schuelerhilfe.de
/gute-noten
CODE   5489

bearbeitet am   **zu erreichende Punktzahl: 14**   **erreichte Punktzahl des Schülers**

➡ Ab **11** erreichten Punkten kannst du zum nächsten Test übergehen.

Test 2 — Present Perfect – simple form

Schwierigkeits-
grad

A 1 Fülle die Tabelle mit den richtigen Formen des *Present Prefects* aus. | 10

positive	negative	question
a) We have won.		
b)	Paul has not spent money.	
c)		Has my wife paid the bill?
d)		Have I lost my keys?
e)	I have not spoken.	

A 2 Schreibe die Fragen ins *Present Perfect* um. | 7

a) Does the teacher correct my mistakes?

....

b) Does my mother buy a new car?

....

c) Does the train leave the station?

....

d) Does my neighbour sell his old car?

....

e) Do they clean up the kitchen?

....

f) Does the goalkeeper catch the ball?

....

g) Does the baby cry?

....

oder:
www.schuelerhilfe.de
/gute-noten
CODE 5489

bearbeitet am _____   zu erreichende Punktzahl: 17   erreichte Punktzahl des Schülers

➡ Ab **14** erreichten Punkten kannst du zum nächsten Test übergehen.

Test 3   Present Perfect – simple form

Schwierigkeits-
grad

A1   Entscheide, ob *Simple Past* oder *Present Perfect* in die Lücken passt.   15

a) I .... *(to eat)* two apples. Now I am full.

b) I .... *(to lose)* my purse!

c) We .... *(to go)* to the cinema last night.

d) We .... *(not to do)* something after school.

e) She .... *(not to read)* about thousand books.

f) He .... *(to watch)* a film yesterday.

g) You .... *(to travel)* to New York. Now you are back.

h) They .... *(to see)* a lot of pigeons.

i) She .... *(to drive)* me home last night.

j) I .... *(not to spend)* so much money.

k) We .... *(not to hide)* from the police.

l) They .... *(to teach)* good lessons.

m) He .... *(to dance)* all night. Now he is tired.

n) You .... *(to write)* an essay two weeks ago.

o) I .... *(to learn)* for the exams well. Now I am ready.

A2   Ordne die Satzbausteine so an, dass ein korrekter englischer Satz entsteht.   7
Setze die Verben in die richtige Zeit *(Simple Present, Simple Past* oder *Present Perfect).*

a) to go · to Anna · I · yesterday · at nine o' clock

....

b) Anna · to bake · a · cake · very delicious · , · now · it · to eat · we

....

c) , · in the garden · to work · they · the whole day · to be · now · they · tired

....

d) one hour ago · to drive · I · to your house

....

e) passport · you · in the kitchen · to see · ? · my

....

f) it · not to see · there · I

....

g) even · not to be · in the house · just · to arrive · I · , · I

....

bearbeitet am [   ]   zu erreichende Punktzahl: 22   erreichte Punktzahl des Schülers [   ]

➡ Ab **18** erreichten Punkten kannst du zum nächsten Test übergehen.

Test 4 — Present Perfect Progressive

Schwierigkeitsgrad

A1 Schreibe die Sätze im *Present Perfect Progressive.*   15

a) I *(to play)* video games all night.

b) She *(to teach)* English in a foreign country.

c) You *(to call)* me this morning.

d) We *(to work)* one month for our presentation.

e) He *(to compose)* three pieces of good classic music.

f) You *(to weaken)* all of us.

g) We *(to plan)* like fools.

h) They *(to use)* wrong materials.

i) It *(to produce)* a huge amount of products.

j) Theodor *(to manage)* the crises and criminals of our jail.

k) I *(to exercise)* all night.

A2 Bilde zu den Sätzen die Verneinung bzw. die Frage.   4

a) You have been watching a film. *(negative)*

b) I have been losing my grammar skills! *(question)*

c) She has been waiting for a long time. *(question)*

d) We have been sailing on a very huge shipper. *(negative)*

oder:
www.schuelerhilfe.de
/gute-noten
CODE 6349

bearbeitet am ___ zu erreichende Punktzahl: 15 erreichte Punktzahl des Schülers ___

➡ Ab **12** erreichten Punkten kannst du zum nächsten Test übergehen.

Test 5 Present Perfect Progressive

Schwierigkeits-grad

A 1 Fülle die Tabelle mit den richtigen Formen des *Present Perfect Progressive* aus. 14

positive	negative	question
a)		Have I been asking something?
b) They have been meeting.		
c)	She has not been cutting.	
d) We have been tearing.		
e)		Have you been noticing?
f) He has been repeating.		
g) It has been diving.		

A 2 Bilde mithilfe der Wörter je eine Aussage, Verneinung und Frage 12
im *Present Perfect Progressive.*

a) I / *(to listen to)* / you

➡ .... ➡ ....

➡ ....

b) *(to use)* / a dictionary / he

➡ .... ➡ ....

➡ ....

c) around the garden / they / *(to go)*

➡ .... ➡ ....

➡ ....

d) *(to give up)* / we

➡ .... ➡ ....

➡ ....

e) you / in hospital / *(to practice)*

➡ .... ➡ ....

➡ ....

f) with Clementine / Carla / *(to disagree)*

➡ .... ➡ ....

➡ ....

oder:
www.schuelerhilfe.de
/gute-noten
CODE 6349

bearbeitet am .... zu erreichende Punktzahl: 26 erreichte Punktzahl des Schülers ....

➡ Ab **21** erreichten Punkten kannst du zum nächsten Test übergehen.

Test **6**   Present Perfect Progressive

Schwierigkeits-
grad

A 1   Ergänze das Gespräch. Entscheide, welche Zeitform *(Simple Present, Simple Past, Present Perfect, Present Perfect Progressive)* die richtige ist.

18

a) The journalist: "Welcome, Charley. Excuse me. _____ for a long time?" *(you / to wait)*

b) Charley Darn: "Good morning. No, _____ *(I / only / to wait)* for five minutes."

c) The journalist: "Good. So, _____ *(you / to immigrate)* to Germany?"

d) Charley Darn: "Yes, _____ *(I / to immigrate)* five years ago."

e) The journalist: "Oh really? And _____ *(you / to participate)* in a project for cultures?"

f) Charley Darn: "Yes, the project is called "Intercontinental Hugs". Up to now _____

    (it / to have) such nice results."

g) The journalist: "_____ *(You / also / to write)* a book, which _____

    (you / to publish) recently: A fantasy of "one world, no borders"?"

h) Charley Darn: "_____ *(I / to be)* in a mood of very specific vision."

i) The journalist: "And there _____ *(the idea / to come up)* for your project?"

j) Charley Darn: "Yes, _____ *(we / to think of)* something like a group around the

    world for cultural exchange."

k) The journalist: "Very nice. So _____ *(we / to hope)* that _____

    (your ideas / to anticipate) worldwide and _____ *(I / to see)* that

    _____ *(you / to record)* a soundtrack, which I am going to listen to right af-

    ter this nice conversation."

l) Charley Darn: "In fact, _____ *(we / to do)*. Thank you. _____

    (it / to be) a nice conversation."

m) The journalist: "Thank you. _____ *(it / to be)* an interesting interview!"

oder:
www.schuelerhilfe.de
/gute-noten
CODE   6349

bearbeitet am _____   **zu erreichende Punktzahl: 18**   **erreichte Punktzahl des Schülers** _____

➡ Ab **14** erreichten Punkten kannst du zum nächsten Test übergehen.

© ZGS Bildungs-GmbH   *Englisch 7/8* • **12**

Test 7 — Present Perfect Simple und Present Perfect Progressive im Vergleich

Schwierigkeits-grad

A1 Wandle die infinitive in die Form des *Present Perfect Simple* um. | 8

a) *(to)* take ➡ ....

b) *(to)* like ➡ ....

c) *(to)* drive ➡ ....

d) *(to)* see ➡ ....

e) *(to)* play ➡ ....

f) *(to)* speak ➡ ....

g) *(to)* put ➡ ....

h) *(to)* meet ➡ ....

A2 Wandle die infinitive in die Form des *Present Perfect Progressive* um. | 8

a) *(to)* write ➡ ....

b) *(to)* talk ➡ ....

c) *(to)* show ➡ ....

d) *(to)* laugh ➡ ....

e) *(to)* cry ➡ ....

f) *(to)* watch ➡ ....

g) *(to)* eat ➡ ....

h) *(to)* drink ➡ ....

A4 Vervollständige die Sätze. Entscheide, ob du *Present Perfect Simple* oder *Present Perfect Progressive* verwenden musst. | 6

a) My father *(never / to drink)* any alcohol.

....

b) The children *(to play)* videogames for three hours.

....

c) You're late. I *(to wait)* for a long time.

....

d) How long *(to know)* your best friend?

....

e) He *(to study)* maths for hours.

....

f) *(She / to work)* hard today?

....

oder:
www.schuelerhilfe.de
/gute-noten
CODE 9119

bearbeitet am [   ] **zu erreichende Punktzahl: 22** **erreichte Punktzahl des Schülers** [   ]

➡ Ab **18** erreichten Punkten kannst du zum nächsten Test übergehen.

Test 8   **Present Perfect Simple und Present Perfect Progressive im Vergleich**

Schwierigkeits-
grad

A1   **Entscheide, welche der beiden Formen richtig ist. Kreuze an.**   `2`

a) Ich möchte erzählen, was ich bis eben gemacht habe.

☐ I have been talking to her.
☐ I have talked to her.

b) Ich möchte mehr das Ergebnis der Handlung als den Verlauf betonen.

☐ She has read a book.
☐ She has been reading a book.

A2   **Schreibe die Sätze in der entsprechenden Form auf.**   `4`

a) I *(to talk)*:

simple form ➡ ....

progressive form ➡ ....

b) He *(to put)*:

simple form ➡ ....

progressive form ➡ ....

c) You *(to eat)*:

simple form ➡ ....

progressive form ➡ ....

d) They *(to drive)*:

simple form ➡ ....

progressive form ➡ ....

A3   **Setze entweder die *Progressive*-Form oder die *Simple*-Form des *Present Perfect* ein.**

a) My team *(lose / only)* two matches so far.

....

b) He *(finish / just)* his homework.

....

c) I *(meet)* three friends this week.

....

d) How long *(wait / you)* for me?

....

e) She *(play)* this game this game since three o'clock.

....

oder:
www.schuelerhilfe.de
/gute-noten
CODE   `9119`

bearbeitet am   **zu erreichende Punktzahl: 11**   **erreichte Punktzahl des Schülers**

➡ Ab **9** erreichten Punkten kannst du zum nächsten Test übergehen.

LE 1: Die Zeiten – Das Present Perfect

Test 9 — Present Perfect Simple und Present Perfect Progressive im Vergleich

Schwierigkeits-grad

A1 Schreibe die folgenden Sätze in beiden Formen auf. 1): *simple form*, 2): *progressive form*. | 12

a) He *(to drink)* coke all day.

1) .... 2) ....

b) I *(not clean)* the kitchen.

1) .... 2) ....

c) They *(to discuss)* all day.

1) .... 2) ....

d) She *(to think)* about it.

1) .... 2) ....

e) We *(to talk)* about you.

1) .... 2) ....

f) She *(to live)* in Germany, since she was seven years old.

1) .... 2) ....

A2 Entscheide dich für die richtige Form und kreuze diese an. | 6

a) She *(has just arrived ☐ / has just been arriving ☐)* at work.

b) He *(has not eaten ☐ / has not been eating ☐)* fish all day.

c) I *(have found ☐ / have been finding ☐)* a new job.

d) He *(has cut ☐ / has been cutting ☐)* his hair.

e) They *(have travelled ☐ / have been travelling ☐)* around Munich all day.

f) My grandpa *(has stopped ☐ / has been stopping ☐)* drinking.

oder:
www.schuelerhilfe.de
/gute-noten
CODE 9119

bearbeitet am _____ zu erreichende Punktzahl: 18 erreichte Punktzahl des Schülers _____

➡ Ab **14** erreichten Punkten kannst du zum nächsten Test übergehen.

Die Zeiten – Das Past Perfect

Test 10 Past Perfect Simple

Schwierigkeits-
grad

A1 Setze die Verben ins *Past Perfect*.

15

a) *(to)* read ➡ ....

b) *(to)* talk ➡ ....

c) *(to)* do ➡ ....

d) *(to)* speak ➡ ....

e) *(to)* look ➡ ....

f) *(to)* cook ➡ ....

g) *(to)* argue ➡ ....

h) *(to)* discuss ➡ ....

i) *(to)* love ➡ ....

j) *(to)* make ➡ ....

k) *(to)* drink ➡ ....

l) *(to)* eat ➡ ....

m) *(to)* buy ➡ ....

n) *(to)* drive ➡ ....

o) *(to)* listen ➡ ....

A2 Entscheide, ob die Verbformen in den Sätzen richtig oder falsch sind und korrigiere sie, wenn nötig.

4

		right	wrong	correction
a)	They talked about the movie they have watched.	☐	☐	
b)	We lived in the house that my grandpa had built.	☐	☐	
c)	I was late for school because I had missed the train.	☐	☐	
d)	I was sad because I has argued with my friend.	☐	☐	

oder:
www.schuelerhilfe.de
/gute-noten
CODE 0441

bearbeitet am [   ]   zu erreichende Punktzahl: 19   erreichte Punktzahl des Schülers [   ]

➡ Ab **15** erreichten Punkten kannst du zum nächsten Test übergehen.

LE 2: Die Zeiten – Das Past Perfect

Schwierigkeits-
grad

A1   **Wandle die Verben ins *Past Perfect* um. Verwende wenn nötig die verneinte Kurzform.**   6

a)   not / to visit   ➡ ....

b)   to put   ➡ ....

c)   to ride   ➡ ....

d)   not / to travel   ➡ ....

e)   to get   ➡ ....

f)   not / to find   ➡ ....

A2   **Vervollständige die Sätze im *Past Perfect*.**   7

a)   We won the match because we *(to practise)* .... the days before.

b)   We were at a restaurant because I *(to be)* .... hungry.

c)   In the supermarket I met a friend who I *(not / to see)* .... for a long time.

d)   Who *(to live)* .... in this flat before we moved in?

e)   You cleaned the kitchen after your mother *(to come)* .... home.

f)   My sister ate all of the cookies that my father *(to make)* ....

g)   She *(never / to see)* .... a lion before that day.

A3   **Bringe die Wörter in die richtige Reihenfolge.**   5

a)   when / arrived / I / the / at / cinema / the / started / had / film

....

b)   had / listened / me / if / you / to / you / have / passed / the / exam / would

....

c)   she / him / met / had / somewhere / before

....

d)   he / studied / lot / a / exam / the / for / had

....

e)   she / hadn't / homework / done / her / so / in / trouble / she / was

....

oder:
www.schuelerhilfe.de
/gute-noten
CODE   0441

bearbeitet am   **zu erreichende Punktzahl: 18**   **erreichte Punktzahl des Schülers**

➡ Ab **14** erreichten Punkten kannst du zum nächsten Test übergehen.

Test 12 — Past Perfect Simple

Schwierigkeitsgrad

A1 **Kreuze die richtige Form des *Past Perfects* an.** — 5

a) to eat / he:

☐ he had eaten ☐ he had ate

b) to dance / she:

☐ she has dance ☐ she had danced

c) to play / they:

☐ they have played ☐ they had played

d) to cook / we:

☐ we had cooked ☐ we have cooked

e) to find / they:

☐ they had found ☐ they have found

A2 **Vervollständige die Sätze mit dem *Past Perfect Simple*.** — 5

a) He told me that he .... *(to buy)* presents for Christmas.

b) She told me that she .... *(to like)* the party on New Year's Eve.

c) They .... *(to be)* in Australia before.

d) We .... *(to know)* him.

e) You cried because your dog .... *(to die)*.

A3 **Übersetze ins Englische und verwende das *Past Perfect*.** — 6

a) Er hatte mit seinem Freund gelacht.

....

b) Wir hatten mit ihm getrunken.

....

c) Sie hatte mit ihr gesungen.

....

d) Du hattest mir das gesagt.

....

e) Er hatte gespielt.

....

f) Ihr hattet gekocht.

....

oder:
www.schuelerhilfe.de
/gute-noten
CODE 0441

bearbeitet am .... zu erreichende Punktzahl: 16 erreichte Punktzahl des Schülers ....

➡ Ab **13** erreichten Punkten kannst du zum nächsten Test übergehen.

Test **13** Past Perfect Progressive

Schwierigkeits-
grad

A1 **Setze die Verben ins *Past Perfect Progressive*.** 11

a) to see ➥ ....

b) to look ➥ ....

c) to drive ➥ ....

d) to show ➥ ....

e) to know ➥ ....

f) to drink ➥ ....

g) to eat ➥ ....

h) to talk ➥ ....

i) to watch ➥ ....

j) to apply ➥ ....

k) to wash ➥ ....

A2 **Kreuze die richtige Form des *Past Perfect Progressive* an.** 6

a) She / ride:

1) ☐ She has been riding 2) ☐ She had been riding

b) He / read:

1) ☐ He had been reading 2) ☐ He have been reading

c) We / clean:

1) ☐ We had been cleaning 2) ☐ We have been cleaning

d) They / travel:

1) ☐ They have been travelling 2) ☐ They had been travelling

e) He / cry:

1) ☐ He had been crying 2) ☐ He has been crying

f) She / laugh:

1) ☐ She has been laughing 2) ☐ She had been laughing

bearbeitet am _____ zu erreichende Punktzahl: 17 erreichte Punktzahl des Schülers _____

➥ Ab **14** erreichten Punkten kannst du zum nächsten Test übergehen.

Test **14**   Past Perfect Progressive

Schwierigkeits-
grad

A1   Entscheide, ob die Verbform richtig oder falsch ist und berichtige, wenn nötig.   7

		right	wrong	correction
a)	had been sleeping	☐	☐	
b)	had been laughed	☐	☐	
c)	had been watched	☐	☐	
d)	had been cleaning	☐	☐	
e)	has been shaking	☐	☐	
f)	have been playing	☐	☐	
g)	had been staying	☐	☐	

A2   Bringe die Wörter in die richtige Reihenfolge.   5

a)   had / sleeping / she / been / 10 / hours / for / when / woke / her / up / you

....

b)   watching / TV / they / had / for / minutes / 30 / been / when / arrived / you

....

c)   he / been / learning / French / had / before / to / he / went / Paris / how / long

....

d)   waiting / bus / for / 10 / minutes / we / had / been / the / for / when / it / started / to / rain

....

e)   he / reading / comic / had / been / a / when / his / came / mother / in

....

A3   Forme die Sätze ins *Past Perfect Progressive* um.   6

a)   The cat eats a fish. ....

b)   The dog drinks water. ....

c)   They play football. ....

d)   We celebrate together. ....

e)   You learn German. ....

f)   She cleans the kitchen. ....

oder:
www.schuelerhilfe.de
/gute-noten
CODE   5265

bearbeitet am ....   zu erreichende Punktzahl: 18   erreichte Punktzahl des Schülers ....

➡ Ab **14** erreichten Punkten kannst du zum nächsten Test übergehen.

© ZGS Bildungs-GmbH   *Englisch 7/8* • 20

LE 2: Die Zeiten – Das Past Perfect

Test 15 Past Perfect Progressive

Schwierigkeits-
grad

A 1 **Wandle die Sätze ins *Past Perfect Progressive* um.** 8

a) He washes his new car.

....

b) She rides her bike.

....

c) They eat a pizza.

....

d) I cook spaghetti.

....

e) The dog looks out the window.

....

f) The cat plays with a mouse.

....

g) The baby sleeps.

....

h) Grandma reads a book.

....

A 2 **Setze die richtige Form in die Lücken ein.** 5

a) Lara .... *(to visit)* her brother all morning.

b) Tom .... *(to speak)* to his teacher.

c) The teacher .... *(to answer)* the questions.

d) We .... *(to take)* photos at the zoo.

e) They .... *(to eat)* at the restaurant.

A 3 **Bilde Fragen im *Past Perfect Progressive*.** 3

a) She · feel · good

.... ?

b) They · live · Cologne

.... ?

c) The policemen · the thief · catch

.... ?

oder:
www.schuelerhilfe.de
/gute-noten
CODE 5265

bearbeitet am .... **zu erreichende Punktzahl: 16** **erreichte Punktzahl des Schülers** ....

➡ Ab **13** erreichten Punkten kannst du zum nächsten Test übergehen.

Test **16** Verwendung von Past Perfect Simple und Past Perfect Progressive

Schwierigkeits-
grad

A1 Welche Signalwörter stehen für das *Past Perfect?* Kreuze die richtigen Antworten an.   `2`

a) ☐ after

b) ☐ always

c) ☐ sometimes

d) ☐ before

e) ☐ usually

f) ☐ yesterday

A2 Kreuze die richtigen Aussagen an.   `4`

a) ☐ Das *Past Perfect* steht für eine Handlung in der Vergangenheit, die vor einer anderen Handlung stattgefunden hat.

b) ☐ Beim *Past Perfect Progressive* wird die Dauer der Handlung in der Vergangenheit betont.

c) ☐ Das *Past Perfect* wird wie folgt gebildet: have + 3. Verbform

d) ☐ Sätze im *Past Perfect Progressive* werden wie folgt gebildet: had + been + Infinitiv + -ing

e) ☐ Der jeweils zweite Satzteil beim *Past Perfect* und *Past Perfect Progressive* steht im Simple Past.

f) ☐ *Past Perfect* = Verlaufsform

A3 Setze folgende Verben ins *Past Perfect.*   `4`

a) 3. Person Singular weiblich · to win

b) 1. Person Plural · to swim

c) 2. Person Singular · to call

d) 3. Person Singular männlich · to catch

oder:
www.schuelerhilfe.de
/gute-noten
CODE `4666`

bearbeitet am ___   **zu erreichende Punktzahl: 10**   **erreichte Punktzahl des Schülers** ___

➡ Ab **8** erreichten Punkten kannst du zum nächsten Test übergehen.

Test 17 Verwendung von Past Perfect Simple und Past Perfect Progressive

Schwierigkeits-
grad

A1 **Welche Sätze stehen im *Past Perfect Simple*. Kreuze die richtigen Antworten an.**   4

a) ☐ My brothers talked about the movie they had seen on DVD.

b) ☐ I'll move to the USA.

c) ☐ When I was younger, I used to play football with my friends Simon and Peter.

d) ☐ I am going to wash my bike tomorrow.

e) ☐ My husband drove me to the hospital because I had fallen out of the window.

f) ☐ I was late at home because I had missed the bus.

g) ☐ My sister had been learning maths for hours when I came home from school.

h) ☐ I wasn't tired because I had been sleeping for 12 hours.

i) ☐ I woke up because my dog had jumped on my bed.

A2 **Vervollständige die Sätze und verwende das *Past Perfect Progressive*.**   7

a) I .... *(to wait)* for 3 hours before my dad picked me up.

b) My mum .... *(to work)* in the backyard for 5 hours before it started to rain.

c) .... *(to sleep / you)* all day before I came home?

d) I .... *(to carry)* my daughter for 30 minutes before she fell asleep.

e) My little sister .... *(to phone)* to her new boyfriend all morning.

f) I .... *(not to speak)* with my friend Magdalena for 2 years.

g) My friend .... *(to write)* a letter for one hour.

oder:
www.schuelerhilfe.de
/gute-noten
CODE   4666

bearbeitet am   zu erreichende Punktzahl: 11   erreichte Punktzahl des Schülers

➡ Ab **9** erreichten Punkten kannst du zum nächsten Test übergehen.

Test 18 Verwendung von Past Perfect Simple und Past Perfect Progressive

Schwierigkeits-
grad

A 1 Bilde Sätze bzw. Fragen und verwende das *Past Perfect Simple.*   5

a) storm · to destroy · fence · we · to build · that · the · green

The ....

b) cookies · to eat · brother · I · the · all · to make · him · for

My ....

c) 2015 · USA · to be · in · the · before · not

I ....

d) bus · to arrive · the · you · to leave · before

.... ?

e) you · with · the · in · garden · to play · dog · the · before · it · to start · to · rain

.... ?

A 2 Bilde Sätze bzw. Fragen und verwende das *Past Perfect Progressive.*   5

a) garden · to sit · you · in · the · when · to ring · bell · the

.... ?

b) not · in · five · London · to live · years · for

I ....

c) the · for · to wait · waiter · 30 · minutes · for

We ....

d) to fly · around · birds · when · their · them · to give · food · human · their

The ....

e) my · to look · for · jeans · morning · all · before · I · to go · to · the · supermarket

I ....

oder:
www.schuelerhilfe.de
/gute-noten
CODE   4666

bearbeitet am ....   zu erreichende Punktzahl: 10   erreichte Punktzahl des Schülers

➡ Ab **8** erreichten Punkten kannst du zum nächsten Test übergehen.

Die Zeiten – Das Futur

Test 19   Simple Present with future meaning

Schwierigkeits-
grad

A 1   **Vervollständige die Sätze mit den Verben in Klammern.**   4

a) The train .... *(leave)* at 6 pm.

b) We .... *(arrive)* in London at 4 pm by bus.

c) Tim's and John's new job .... *(start)* on Friday.

d) The cinema .... *(open)* on Tuesday.

A 2   **Die nachfolgenden Verben weisen alle auf die Verwendung des *Simple Present with future meaning* hin, aber es haben sich zwei nicht dazugehörende Verben eingeschlichen. Streiche die falschen Verben durch und umkreise die richtigen Verben.**   8

a) arrive

b) give

c) close

d) end

e) fly

f) think

g) open

h) leave

A 3   **Welche der nachfolgenden Aussagen ist richtig? Kreuze an.**   1

Das *Simple Present with future meaning* wird genutzt, ...

a) ☐ wenn man über ein Ereignis in der Gegenwart spricht.

b) ☐ wenn man über ein Ereignis in der Zukunft spricht, welches nicht geplant ist und auch nicht sicher feststeht.

c) ☐ wenn man über ein Ereignis in der Zukunft spricht, welches durch einen Fahrplan oder ein Programm festgelegt ist.

oder:
www.schuelerhilfe.de
/gute-noten
CODE 4734

---

bearbeitet am   zu erreichende Punktzahl: 13   erreichte Punktzahl des Schülers

➡ Ab **10** erreichten Punkten kannst du zum nächsten Test übergehen.

LE 3: Die Zeiten – Das Futur

Test 20 Simple Present with future meaning

Schwierigkeits-grad

A 1 **Ergänze die nachfolgenden Sätze richtig.** | 3 |

a) What time .... the train .... (leave) this evening?

b) My bus .... (not arrive) at 8.30 pm, it .... (arrive) at 8.30 pm.

c) The Millers .... (not leave) at 10 pm by bus, they .... (leave) at 11 pm.

A 2 **Unterstreiche in den nachfolgenden Sätzen den Hinweis, der darauf hindeutet, dass man das *Simple Present with future meaning* nutzen sollte.** | 6 |

a) The bus leaves tomorrow at 8 o'clock.

b) Peter goes on a weekend trip with his football team next weekend.

c) The train arrives at 6:30 in the morning.

d) Jenny has a yoga class on Wednesday in the morning.

e) Next Friday at 12 o'clock there is an important Spanish exam.

f) The plane leaves in 15 minutes.

A 3 **Ergänze die Lücken in den nachfolgenden Sätzen richtig.** | 6 |

a) Peter .... (take) the train at 7:30 pm tomorrow.

b) My English class .... (start) at 8 o'clock every Monday.

c) The train .... (not leave) at 3 o'clock because of technical problems.

d) The competition .... (begin) this weekend.

e) .... the plane .... (leave) London at 2 o'clock tonight?

f) Tom .... (have) his football training at 6:30 tomorrow and not as usual at 7:00.

oder:
www.schuelerhilfe.de
/gute-noten
CODE   4734

bearbeitet am .... **zu erreichende Punktzahl: 15** **erreichte Punktzahl des Schülers**

➡ Ab **12** erreichten Punkten kannst du zum nächsten Test übergehen.

Test **21** Simple Present with future meaning

Schwierigkeits-
grad

A1 **Ist die Lösung jeweils richtig oder falsch?** 5

Hinweise für das *Simple Present with future meaning* im Satz sind:

a) Fahrpläne ....

b) feste Termine ....

c) vage Umschreibungen ....

d) ungenaue Zeitaussagen ....

e) festes Programm ....

A2 **Fülle die jeweiligen Lücken mit der richtigen Form des Verbs im Satz für** 6
das *Simple Present with future meaning.*

a) The train .... *(arrive)* at 7 pm.

b) On Monday our new teacher for mathematics .... *(have)* her first day at work.

c) .... the gym .... *(open)* at 8:00 am or at 8:30 am?

d) The plane to Amsterdam .... *(leave)* in 15 minutes and Jenny is still not at the airport.

e) The opening of the new club in the city .... *(begin)* at 11 pm on Friday.

f) My bus always .... *(arrive)* at my bus stop 5 minutes earlier than expected.

oder:
www.schuelerhilfe.de
/gute-noten
CODE 4734

bearbeitet am **zu erreichende Punktzahl: 11** **erreichte Punktzahl des Schülers**

➡ Ab **9** erreichten Punkten kannst du zum nächsten Test übergehen.

Test 22 Present Progressive with future meaning

Schwierigkeits-
grad

A1 **Sind die folgenden Aussagen richtig oder falsch? Entscheide.** 4

Das *Present Progressive with future meaning* ...

a) ... benutzt man um über Handlungen zu reden, die für die (nähere) Zukunft geplant sind.

b) ... benutzt man nie.

c) ... wird durch Signalwörter angedeutet. Diese sind zum Beispiel: *on Sunday, next Friday, tomorrow oder at the weekend.*

d) ... beschreibt ungenaue Ideen für die ferne Zukunft.

A2 **Ergänze die Lücken in den Sätzen und nutze dafür die Verben aus der Tabelle.** 6

am winning · is meeting · is going · is flying · are eating · are taking

a) Tom .... Sarah tomorrow.

b) On Sunday Sam .... from Germany to Rome to visit his sister.

c) We .... the train to Berlin next week.

d) They .... in the new restaurant on Friday.

e) Olivia .... to the new shop tomorrow.

f) I .... the competition on Thursday.

A3 **Unterstreiche die Signalwörter, die auf das *Present Progressive with future meaning* hinweisen.** 5

a) We are going to the basketball match tomorrow.

b) On Wednesday I am leaving school earlier.

c) Next week Sarah is taking the train to visit her friend in Munich.

d) School is ending an hour later on Friday because of an event.

e) My friends are visiting me in hospital on Saturday.

oder:
www.schuelerhilfe.de
/gute-noten
CODE 9618

bearbeitet am .... zu erreichende Punktzahl: 15 erreichte Punktzahl des Schülers ....

➡ Ab **12** erreichten Punkten kannst du zum nächsten Test übergehen.

Test 23 Present Progressive with future meaning

Schwierigkeits-
grad

A1 Ergänze die nachfolgenden Sätze richtig. 8

a) Tom .... *(not leave)* London next week.

b) What .... you .... *(do)* on Saturday evening?

c) I .... *(visit)* Sam for the the first time this weekend on Friday.

d) What time .... you .... *(leave)*?

e) When exactly .... she .... *(meet)* her parents this evening?

f) On Sunday morning Luke and Lea .... *(take)* photos of some sights in London.

g) They .... *(not visit)* the wax museum today.

h) Susan .... *(make)* plans for the next weekend.

A2 Kreuze den richtigen Satz an. 4

a) ☐ On Thursday afternoon Charlotte is taking the train from Bochum to Bonn.
    ☐ Last Thursday afternoon Charlotte is taking the train from Bochum to Bonn.

b) ☐ In the morning Bernd is helping his grandma with her household.
    ☐ In two weeks in the morning Bernd is helping is grandma with her household.

c) ☐ Alisa usually works on Mondays.
    ☐ Alisa usually is working on Mondays.

d) ☐ At noon they are having lunch later today.
    ☐ At noon they had lunch later today.

oder:
www.schuelerhilfe.de
/gute-noten
CODE 9618

bearbeitet am   zu erreichende Punktzahl: 12   erreichte Punktzahl des Schülers

➡ Ab **10** erreichten Punkten kannst du zum nächsten Test übergehen.

Test 24   Present Progressive with future meaning

Schwierigkeits-
grad

A1   Verbinde die jeweils zusammengehörigen Satzteile und setze in die Lücken | 7 |
das *Present Progressive with future meaning* ein.

1. On Saturday Jim .... *(get up)*
2. He .... *(not have)*
3. Jim's two sisters Sarah and Paula .... *(meet)*
4. His friend Josh .... *(not come)*
5. They .... *(go)*
6. At 7:30 pm they .... *(play)*
7. Later his co-player Adam .... *(invite)*

a) all the other players to his house.
b) to his house at 12.30 pm because he is late.
c) to the basketball match all together by the bus.
d) at 7:00 am in the morning.
e) against a very good team from Liverpool.
f) him at 9:00 am for breakfast in his kitchen.
g) breakfast with his mother as usual because she is already working.

A2   Übersetze und verwende das *Present Progressive with future meaning.* | 5 |

a) Morgen werde ich in die Stadt gehen um neue Kleidung zu kaufen.

....

b) Nächste Woche werde ich meinen Onkel in Amerika besuchen.

....

c) Carol und Tim werden nächste Woche den Zug nach Berlin nehmen.

....

d) Wir werden am Montag mit unserer Klasse ein Museum in Amsterdam besuchen.

....

e) Er wird am Samstag arbeiten, aber das ist kein Problem, weil ich alleine etwas unternehmen kann.

....

oder:
www.schuelerhilfe.de
/gute-noten
CODE   9618

bearbeitet am | | **zu erreichende Punktzahl: 12**   **erreichte Punktzahl des Schülers** | |

➡ Ab **10** erreichten Punkten kannst du zum nächsten Test übergehen.

Test 25 Das *going to*-future

Schwierigkeits-
grad

A1 Vervollständige die Lücken. 6

a) I .... going to write a letter to my uncle.

b) You .... going to see your relatives this weekend.

c) He .... going to do his homework this afternoon.

d) She .... going to sing the new song at the festival.

e) We .... going to go to the theatre.

f) They .... going to meet in front of Susan's house.

A2 Verneine die folgenden Sätze im *going to-future*. Verwende die Kurzform. 4

a) Sarah is going to write the exam after lunch.

....

b) The neighbours are going to meet for a barbecue.

....

c) My brother is going to play soccer in the garden.

....

d) My classmates are going to study for maths together.

....

A3 Beantworte die folgenden Fragen im *going to-future*. 3

a) Are the Smiths going to visit New York City this summer?

Yes, the Smiths are ....

b) Is dad going to listen to his favourite band tonight?

Yes, dad is ....

c) Are Julia and Stefan going to go to the school ball tonight?

No, Julia and Stefan aren't ....

oder:
www.schuelerhilfe.de
/gute-noten
CODE 9876

bearbeitet am _____   zu erreichende Punktzahl: 13   erreichte Punktzahl des Schülers _____

➡ Ab **10** erreichten Punkten kannst du zum nächsten Test übergehen.

Test 26 Das *going to*-future

Schwierigkeits-
grad

A1 Bilde zu den gegebenen Infinitiven sowohl die positive Form als auch die
verneinte Form im *going to-future*.

5

a) to be   (+)   he ....   (–)   he ....
b) to sleep   (+)   they ....   (–)   they ....
c) to say   (+)   she ....   (–)   she ....
d) to go   (+)   we ....   (–)   we ....
e) to hear   (+)   I ....   (–)   I ....

A2 Leite aus den gegebenen Antworten Fragen im *going to-future* ab.

4

a) Yes, Clara is going to become 15 years this Friday.

.... ?

b) Yes, my grandparents are going to buy a house at the beach.

.... ?

c) No, the children aren't going to win the match against the champion.

.... ?

d) No, the cat isn't going to jump onto the wall.

.... ?

A3 Beantworte die folgenden Fragen im *going to-future*. Nutze Langformen.

4

a) Are you going to pass the exams at the end of the year? (+)

....

b) Is the school going to celebrate an anniversary this autumn? (+)

....

c) Is she going to sing in the choir this semester? (–)

....

d) Is the elephant going to eat fruits for dinner? (–)

....

oder:
www.schuelerhilfe.de
/gute-noten
CODE   9876

bearbeitet am _____   zu erreichende Punktzahl: 13   erreichte Punktzahl des Schülers _____

➡ Ab **10** erreichten Punkten kannst du zum nächsten Test übergehen.

LE 3: Die Zeiten – Das Futur

Test 27   Das *going to*-future

Schwierigkeits-grad

A1   Entscheide, ob die Aussagen über das *going to-future* richtig oder falsch sind. | 4 |

a) The *going-to-future* is used when we want so make a prediction or   ☐ richtig ☐ falsch
an assumption about the future.

b) The *going-to-future* is used to talk about intentions or plans for the future. ☐ richtig ☐ falsch

c) The *going-to-future* is used for spontaneous decisions.   ☐ richtig ☐ falsch

d) The *going-to-future* is built with a form of the auxiliary verb "be"   ☐ richtig ☐ falsch
in the present plus "going to" plus infinitive of the main verb.

A2   Bilde anhand der gegebenen Satzteile Fragen im *going to-future*. | 5 |

a) to do · night · tomorrow · homework · your · you

....?

b) the dishes · when · dad · to wash

....?

c) how/ to solve · the students · the problem

....?

d) the doctor · to call · the hospital

....?

e) to meet · where · the children · this weekend

....?

A3   Setze die Verben in Klammern im *going to-future* ein. | 9 |

a) What .... you .... *(to do)* this evening?

b) Mom .... *(to go)* to her office at 7 o'clock next Monday.

c) Judy's holidays .... *(to be)* planned perfectly.

d) The officer's dog .... *(not / to bark)* loudly.

e) Timothy .... *(to write)* a test in the sports hall this afternoon.

f) My grandparents .... *(not / to stay)* in a hotel when they visit us.

g) .... the plane .... *(to start)* in time?

h) The music festival .... *(to take)* place in Las Vegas.

i) I can tell you that I .... *(to ask)* Jonas for a date.

oder:
www.schuelerhilfe.de
/gute-noten
CODE   9876

bearbeitet am   zu erreichende Punktzahl: 18   erreichte Punktzahl des Schülers

➡ Ab **14** erreichten Punkten kannst du zum nächsten Test übergehen.

LE 3: Die Zeiten – Das Futur

Test 28 Das *will*-future

A 1 Kreuze an, welche Signalwörter auf das *will-future* zutreffen können. `2`

a) ☐ since, for

b) ☐ tomorrow, next month

c) ☐ always, every

d) ☐ last, yesterday

e) ☐ in 2022, the coming year

f) ☐ ever, before

A 2 Setze die richtige Form des *will-futures* ein. Nutze die Verben in Klammern. `6`

a) Julia and I .... to them tomorrow. *(to talk)*

b) .... you .... your father to tidy up the kitchen? *(to help)*

c) They .... back by 8:15 pm. *(to be)*

d) .... the festival .... place this summer? *(to take)*

e) My parents .... me for being late. *(not / to punish)*

f) The Millers .... Christmas in Sussex this year. *(not / to spend)*

A 3 Setze die Kurzform des *will-futures* für die gegebenen Sätze ein. `5`

a) They will read a book. ➡ They .... a book.

b) He will not be late. ➡ He .... late.

c) She will never learn. ➡ She .... never ....

d) We will not sing this song. ➡ We .... this song.

e) I will give you the money. ➡ I .... you the money.

oder:
www.schuelerhilfe.de
/gute-noten
CODE 5659

bearbeitet am .... zu erreichende Punktzahl: 13 erreichte Punktzahl des Schülers ....

➡ Ab **10** erreichten Punkten kannst du zum nächsten Test übergehen.

© ZGS Bildungs-GmbH *Englisch 7/8* ▪ **34**

LE 3: Die Zeiten – Das Futur

Test 29 — Das *will*-future

Schwierigkeits-
grad

A1 Bilde zu den gegebenen Infinitiven sowohl die positive Form als auch die verneinte Form im *will-future*.   5

a) to be   (+) ....   (–) ....

b) to sleep   (+) ....   (–) ....

c) to say   (+) ....   (–) ....

d) to go   (+) ....   (–) ....

e) to hear   (+) ....   (–) ....

A2 Entscheide, ob die Formen des *will-futures* in den Beispielsätzen richtig unterstrichen sind.   6

	richtig	falsch
a) My uncle <u>will come</u> to dinner this evening.	☐	☐
b) <u>Will you</u> spend your holidays in Italy this year?	☐	☐
c) He <u>will</u> never <u>know</u>, <u>will</u> he?	☐	☐
d) You won't <u>leave</u> the room!	☐	☐
e) We <u>will not pass</u> this difficult exam.	☐	☐
f) <u>Will</u> the Turners <u>pay</u> the bill tonight?	☐	☐

A3 Entscheide, ob die Aussagen über das *will-future* richtig oder falsch sind.   5

	richtig	falsch
a) Das *will-future* wird für Vorhersagen und Vermutungen verwendet.	☐	☐
b) Das *will-future* wird durch *will + Infinitiv* gebildet.	☐	☐
c) Für das Hilfsverb *will* gibt es keine Kurzform.	☐	☐
d) Die Langform der Verneinung *will not + Infinitiv* wird zu *won't + Infinitiv* verkürzt.	☐	☐
e) Das *will-future* wird für zukünftige, eindeutig festgelegte Pläne verwendet.	☐	☐

oder:
www.schuelerhilfe.de
/gute-noten
CODE 5659

bearbeitet am   zu erreichende Punktzahl: 16   erreichte Punktzahl des Schülers

➡ Ab **13** erreichten Punkten kannst du zum nächsten Test übergehen.

© ZGS Bildungs-GmbH   *Englisch 7/8* • **35**

Test 30 Das *will*-future

Schwierigkeits-
grad

A1 Entscheide, ob das *will-future* in den Beispielen richtig gebraucht wurde. 6

richtig falsch

a) According to the weather report, it will be cloudy tomorrow. ☐ ☐

b) "Why did you buy this paint?" – "I will paint my room tomorrow." ☐ ☐

c) "Listen! The phone is ringing." – "I'll get it." ☐ ☐

d) Sam has just bought a house in York. He will move on Saturday. ☐ ☐

e) "Here, I will help you carry that box. It looks heavy." ☐ ☐

f) Anna will come tomorrow around 5 o'clock. ☐ ☐

A2 Bilde anhand der vorgegebenen Wörter Fragesätze im *will-future*. 5

a) (it · snow) .... ?

b) (me · she · forgive) .... ?

c) (what · learn · they) .... ?

d) (not · the bus · wait · for us) .... ?

e) (they · leave · when) .... ?

A3 Entscheide, ob das *will-future* in der englischen Übersetzung angebracht ist. 3

richtig falsch

a) Ich schwitze jetzt schon. Es wird heute sehr heiß werden, fürchte ich. ☐ ☐
➡ I'm sweating already. It will be very hot today, I'm afraid.

b) Ich habe ihm einen Brief auf den Tisch hinterlassen. Glaubst du, dass er ihn ☐ ☐
finden wird?
➡ I've left a letter for him on the table. Do you think he'll see it?

c) Früher oder später wird er seinen Fehler bemerken. ☐ ☐
➡ Sooner or later he will realize his mistake.

oder:
www.schuelerhilfe.de
/gute-noten
CODE 5659

bearbeitet am   zu erreichende Punktzahl: 14   erreichte Punktzahl des Schülers

➡ Ab **11** erreichten Punkten kannst du zum nächsten Test übergehen.

Verschiedene Zeiten der Gegenwart und Vergangenheit

Test 31 — Verwendung von Simple Present und Present Progressive

Schwierigkeits-grad

A 1 — Hier stehen verschiedene Bedingungen, die vorgeben, welche Zeitform verwendet werden muss. Ordne das *Simple Present* und *Present Progressive* den Optionen zu. | 9

a) wiederholte Handlungen

b) Veränderungen

c) allgemeine Aussagen

d) Handlungen, die im Moment des Sprechens (jetzt gerade) passieren

e) Anweisungen

f) feststehende Pläne für die Zukunft

g) aufeinanderfolgende Handlungen in der Gegenwart

h) vorübergehende Handlungen

i) feststehende Abläufe

A 2 — Setze das Verb in die angegebene Zeit- und Personenform. | 3

a) 1. Person Singular, Present Progressive von: to feel good

b) 3. Person Singular, Simple Present von: to hurry up

c) 3. Person Plural, Present Progressive von: to lie

A 3 — Fülle die Lücken mit dem Verb in der richtigen Zeitform. | 4

a) Usually, Ben _____ (to finish / not) his homework in time.

b) Right now, Daniel _____ (to wash) the car.

c) Daniel _____ (to want) to finish washing the car, but it takes a long time.

d) What are you doing? – I _____ (to hide) the present under my bed.

oder:
www.schuelerhilfe.de
/gute-noten
CODE 6696

---

bearbeitet am _____   zu erreichende Punktzahl: 16   erreichte Punktzahl des Schülers

➡ Ab **13** erreichten Punkten kannst du zum nächsten Test übergehen.

Test 32 — Verwendung von Simple Present und Present Progressive

Schwierigkeits-
grad

A 1 Hier stehen verschiedene Signalwörter, die vorgeben, welche Zeitform verwendet werden | 12
muss. Ordne das *Simple Present* und *Present Progressive* den Optionen zu.

a) always ....

b) usually ....

c) never ....

d) now ....

e) every week ....

f) Listen! ....

g) at the moment ....

h) on Tuesdays ....

i) seldom ....

j) Look! ....

k) often ....

l) every day ....

A 2 Bringe die Wörter in die richtige Reihenfolge, sodass ein ganzer Satz entsteht. | 3
Achte auf die richtige Zeitform des Verbs.

a) to leave · at · bus · 9:04 am · the · today

....

b) cat · tree · Look! · up · the · the · brown · to climb

....

c) up · brother · please · your · to wake

....

A 3 Finde die Fehler und korrigiere sie. | 3

a) Right now, I do my homework together with my cousin.

....

b) If you notice the light is changeing to green press that button.

....

c) My little brother watchs TV every morning.

....

bearbeitet am .... zu erreichende Punktzahl: 18 erreichte Punktzahl des Schülers

➡ Ab **14** erreichten Punkten kannst du zum nächsten Test übergehen.

Test 33 Verwendung von Simple Present und Present Progressive

Schwierigkeits-
grad

A1 **Beantworte die Fragen mit einem ganzen Satz. Achte auf die richtige Zeitform.** 6

a) How are you feeling right now? *(not well)*

....

b) What lessons do you have today? *(maths – biology – arts)*

....

c) Why is everybody looking outside of the windows? *(to snow)*

....

d) Are you writing your essay right now? *(Yes)*

....

e) Is your dad preparing the duck for Christmas dinner already? *(No)*

....

f) When does the next bus to Berlin leave? *(at 13:00 today)*

....

A2 **Fülle die Lücken mit der richtigen Form des Verbs.** 5

a) Mum .... *(to work)* in the garden while the toddlers .... *(to play)* outside
with the rabbits.

b) Tomorrow, Jim .... *(to cook)* "Chicken Alfredo" for his family. He's already bought the
ingredients.

c) The library .... *(to close)* during the night.

d) Thomas always .... *(to go)* to the bakery on Sundays.

e) While the rice .... *(to boil)*, you must .... *(to chop)* the vegetables.

A3 **Übersetze die Sätze ins Englische. Achte auf die richtige Zeitform des Verbs.** 5

a) Mein Klavierunterricht beginnt heute um 19:00.

....

b) Jetzt wechselt jeder die Straßenseite wegen des gefährlichen Verkehrs.

....

c) Der Lehrer buchstabiert das Wort, damit es jeder aufschreiben kann.

....

d) Heutzutage spielen viele Kinder nicht mehr so oft draußen.

....

e) Kinder unter 16 Jahren dürfen diesen Film noch nicht schauen.

....

oder:
www.schuelerhilfe.de
/gute-noten
CODE 6696

bearbeitet am | **zu erreichende Punktzahl: 16** **erreichte Punktzahl des Schülers**

➡ **Ab 13 erreichten Punkten kannst du zum nächsten Test übergehen.**

Test 34 — Verwendung von Present und Past Progressive

Schwierigkeits-
grad

A1 Hier stehen verschiedene Bedingungen, die vorgeben, welche Zeitform verwendet werden muss. Ordne das *Present Progressive* und *Past Progressive* den Optionen zu. | 7

a) Handlungen, die für die Zukunft bereits abgesprochen sind

....

b) in der Vergangenheit im Ablauf befindliche Handlungen

....

c) im Ablauf befindliche Handlung der Vergangenheit, die durch eine neue Handlung unterbrochen wird

....

d) auf einen bestimmten Zeitraum begrenzte Handlung der Gegenwart

....

e) Handlungen, die sich jetzt gerade im Ablauf befinden

....

f) gleichzeitig ablaufende Handlungen in der Vergangenheit

....

g) Passierendes im Moment des Sprechens

....

A2 Setze das Verb in die angegebene Zeit- und Personenform. | 4

a) 2. Person Singular, Present Progressive von: to check

b) 3. Person Plural, Past Progressive von: to believe

c) 3. Person Singular, Past Progressive von: to die

d) 2. Person Plural, Present Progressive von: to run

A3 Setze das Verb in der richtigen Zeitform in die Lücken ein. | 4

a) Right now, I .... (to cook) dinner for my family.

b) Tomorrow, Sarah .... (to wash) her clothes. Everything is dirty!

c) During that workshop last week we .... (to talk) about body shaming.

d) Tom .... (to tidy up) his room, when his friend Ben entered.

oder:
www.schuelerhilfe.de
/gute-noten
CODE 7633

bearbeitet am .... zu erreichende Punktzahl: 15 erreichte Punktzahl des Schülers

➡ Ab **12** erreichten Punkten kannst du zum nächsten Test übergehen.

Schwierigkeits-
grad

A 1 Hier stehen verschiedene Signalwörter, die vorgeben, welche Zeitform verwendet werden | 9 |
muss. Ordne das *Present Progressive* und *Past Progressive* den Optionen zu.

a) when ....

b) now ....

c) at the moment ....

d) Look! ....

e) while ....

f) presently ....

g) right now ....

h) 1999 ....

i) last week ....

A 2 Verändere die Zeitformen in den Sätzen. Verwandle also Sätze im *Present Progressive* | 4 |
ins *Past Progressive* und umgekehrt. Ändere wenn nötig auch die Signalwörter.

a) Right now, I am searching the internet for a present for my sister.

....

b) Yesterday, Ashley was preparing for her speech at work.

....

c) I am doing my homework at the moment.

....

d) He is flying on the plane while I am at school.

....

A 3 Bringe die Wörter in die richtige Reihenfolge, sodass ein ganzer Satz entsteht. | 4 |
Achte auf die richtige Zeitform des Verbs.

a) to wait · until · mall · the · the · in · to arrive · I · train · now

....

b) about · to talk to · yesterday · my friend · her opinion · to ask · I

....

c) your · already · you · homework · to do · ?

....

d) to feel · right · you · how · now · ?

....

bearbeitet am [ ] zu erreichende Punktzahl: 17 erreichte Punktzahl des Schülers [ ]

➡ Ab **14** erreichten Punkten kannst du zum nächsten Test übergehen.

Test 36 Verwendung von Present und Past Progressive

Schwierigkeits-grad

A1 Beantworte die Fragen mit einem ganzen Satz. Achte auf die richtige Form des Verbs. 5

a) What are you doing right now? *(to watch a movie)*

....

b) Why were you feeling bad yesterday? *(to have bad headache)*

....

c) What were you talking about in class today? *(to do some exercises)*

....

d) What happened while you were eating lunch? *(to start to snow)*

....

e) What is in your bottle? *(to drink apple juice)*

....

A2 Übersetze die Sätze ins Englische. Achte auf die richtige Zeitform des Verbs. 4

a) Während ich ans Telefon ging, kochte die Milch über.

....

b) Ich fühle mich gerade nicht so gut.

....

c) Er kam nach Hause, als Ben gerade den Abwasch machte.

....

d) Nächste Woche fahre ich mit dem Bus nach Hause.

....

A3 Finde die Fehler und korrigiere sie. 5

a) Yesterday, Debbie was tiding up her room.

....

b) Sarah is runing through the forest with her new shoes right now.

....

c) At the moment, I am writting an essay about the 2nd world war.

....

d) Right now, Dan was kissing his girlfriend.

....

e) The singer at the concert last week is singing about his best friend.

....

oder:
www.schuelerhilfe.de
/gute-noten
CODE 7633

bearbeitet am .... zu erreichende Punktzahl: 14 erreichte Punktzahl des Schülers ....

➡ Ab **11** erreichten Punkten kannst du zum nächsten Test übergehen.

Test 37 — Verwendung von Past und Past Perfect

Schwierigkeits-
grad

A1 Hier stehen verschiedene Bedingungen, die vorgeben, welche Zeitform verwendet werden muss. Ordne das *Past Perfect* und *Simple Past* den Beschreibungen zu. — 9

a) Handlung geschah vor einer anderen Handlung in der Vergangenheit

....

b) vergangene Fakten

....

c) beendete Handlung in der Vergangenheit

....

d) Handlung dauerte bis zu einer anderen Handlung in der Vergangenheit

....

e) vergangene Generalisierungen

....

f) Andauerndes in der Vergangenheit

....

g) Gewohnheiten in der Vergangenheit

....

h) einmalige Handlungen in der Vergangenheit

....

i) wiederholte Handlungen in der Vergangenheit

....

A2 Vervollständige die Tabelle mit den Verbformen im *Simple Past* und *Past Perfect*. Achte auf unregelmäßige Formen. — 8

	infinitive	Simple Past	Past Perfect
a)	to go		
b)		put	
c)			had bought
d)	to sell		

oder:
www.schuelerhilfe.de
/gute-noten
CODE 0073

bearbeitet am _____   zu erreichende Punktzahl: 17   erreichte Punktzahl des Schülers _____

➡ Ab **14** erreichten Punkten kannst du zum nächsten Test übergehen.

Test 38 — Verwendung von Past und Past Perfect

Schwierigkeits-grad

A1 Hier stehen verschiedene Signalwörter, die vorgeben, welche Zeitform verwendet werden muss. Ordne das *Past Perfect* und *Simple Past* den Signalwörtern zu. | 10

a) after ....

b) in 1999 ....

c) never ....

d) last Friday ....

e) before 2006 ....

f) yesterday ....

g) two minutes ago ....

h) already ....

i) just ....

j) when ....

A2 Fülle die Lücken mit der richtigen Zeitform des Verbs. | 9

a) Last year I .... *(to travel)* to Spain to visit my best friend.

b) My sister .... *(to start)* baking the birthday cake after she .... *(to do)* the groceries.

c) Before that event last week, my best friend .... *(to never lose)* her passport.

d) Ben and David .... *(to finish)* their homework two hours ago.

e) In 2012, our New Year's Eve .... *(to be)* very boring.

f) After I .... *(to be)* in South America, I .... *(to go)* to the USA.

g) My boyfriend .... *(to use to smoke)* some years ago.

h) He .... *(to never think)* about being in danger in his hometown before 9/11.

i) Last week, Jenny .... *(to see)* a man breaking into her neighbor's house. Before that,

she .... *(to visit)* her best friend Sarah, because she .... *(to feel)* sick.

Afterwards, Jenny .... *(to tell)* Sarah everything.

oder:
www.schuelerhilfe.de
/gute-noten
CODE 0073

bearbeitet am .... zu erreichende Punktzahl: 19 erreichte Punktzahl des Schülers ....

➡ Ab **15** erreichten Punkten kannst du zum nächsten Test übergehen.

Test 39 Verwendung von Past und Past Perfect

Schwierigkeitsgrad

A 1 Schreibe das Verb in der richtigen Zeit- und Personenform auf. 5

a) 1. Person Plural, ***Simple Past*** von: to sit ....

b) 3. Person Plural, ***Past Perfect*** von: to build ....

c) 2. Person Singular, ***Simple Past*** von: to keep ....

d) 1. Person Singular, ***Past Perfect*** von: to study ....

e) 2. Person Plural, ***Past Perfect*** von: to bring ....

A 2 Bringe die Wörter in die richtige Reihenfolge, sodass sie einen Satz ergeben. Achte darauf, dass das Verb in der richtigen Zeitform steht. 7

a) yesterday ▪ it ▪ day ▪ to rain ▪ whole ▪ the

....

b) to start ▪ yet ▪ she ▪ the ▪ project ▪ with ▪ not ▪ two days ago

....

c) to bake ▪ for ▪ I ▪ a cake ▪ tea time ▪ last week's ▪ for

....

d) school ▪ the groceries ▪ he ▪ after ▪ to pick up ▪ his son ▪ to do ▪ from ▪ he

....

e) the windows ▪ the house ▪ you ▪ you ▪ to close ▪ to leave ▪ before ?

....

f) to wait ▪ before ▪ I ▪ you ▪ for ▪ for ▪ the train ▪ I ▪ two hours ▪ home ▪ to take

....

g) Christmas dinner ▪ to taste ▪ last year ▪ very ▪ delicious ▪ our

....

A 3 Übersetze die Sätze ins Englische. Achte auf die richtige Zeitform des Verbs. 3

a) Bist du heute Morgen zum Bäcker gegangen, nachdem du aufgestanden warst?

....

b) Meine beste Freundin hat mir gestern eine interessante Geschichte erzählt.

....

c) Habt ihr das alle richtig verstanden?

....

oder:
www.schuelerhilfe.de
/gute-noten
CODE 0073

bearbeitet am ______ zu erreichende Punktzahl: 15 erreichte Punktzahl des Schülers ______

➨ Ab 12 erreichten Punkten kannst du zum nächsten Test übergehen.

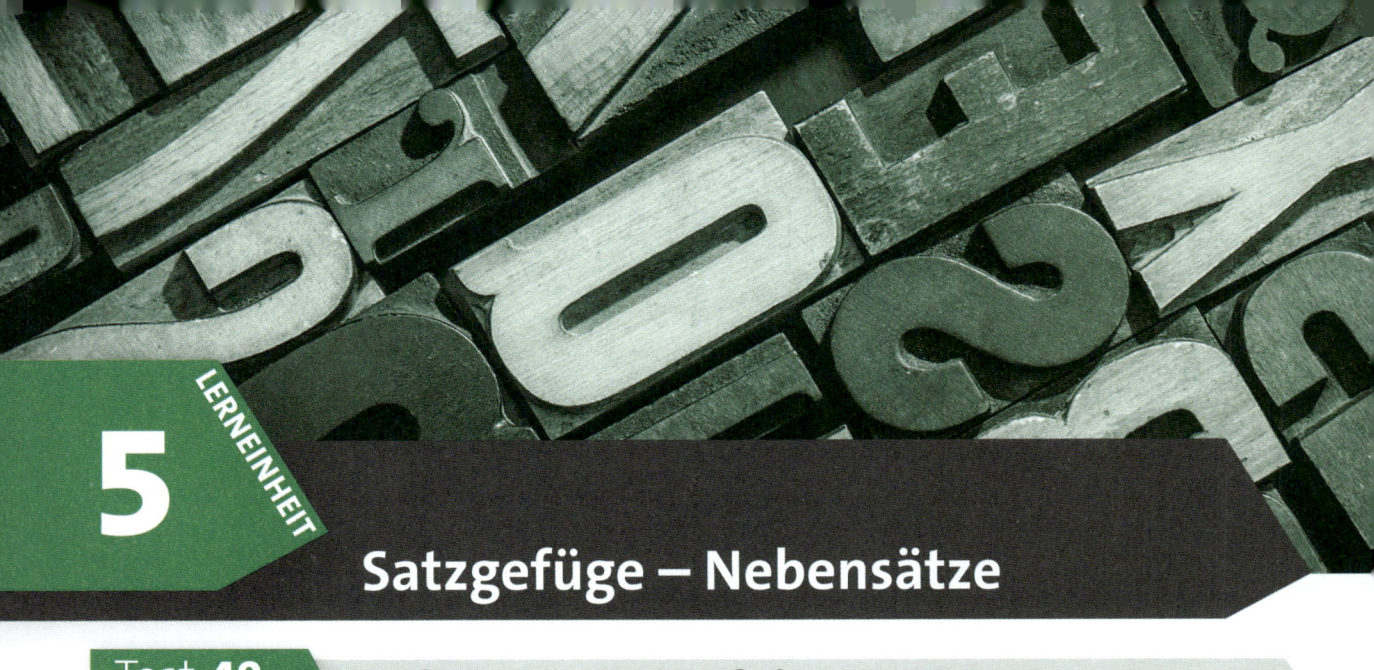

Test 40 Bedingungssätze – if-clauses Typ 1

Schwierigkeits-grad

A1 **Kreuze diejenigen Sätze an, die zu den sogenannten *conditional sentences* gehören.** | 2 |

a) Do you think that the sun will shine today? ☐

b) If the sun shines, we will go to the park. ☐

c) Water freezes, if the temperatures fall below zero. ☐

A2 **Vervollständige die *if-clauses* mit dem Verb in Klammern. Nutze das *Simple Present*.** | 5 |

a) If I .... *(have)* enough time, I will watch TV later this night.

b) Susan will visit her grandmother this afternoon, if she .... *(catch)* the train.

c) If the Smiths .... *(be)* late, they will miss the football game.

d) If Patrick .... *(call)* this afternoon, I will ask him for dinner.

e) We will buy the new CD, if I .... *(find)* my purse.

A3 **Ergänze die folgenden Sätze, indem du dich für eine der vorgegebenen Versionen entscheidest.** | 5 |

a) If I give up smoking, I ☐ will live / ☐ live longer.

b) If they get married, everyone ☐ is / ☐ will be shocked.

c) If the students work harder, I am sure they ☐ will get / ☐ get better marks.

d) If you get the job, they ☐ will call / ☐ call you right away.

e) If you see Professor Clever, you ☐ must ask / ☐ ask him for his new book.

oder:
www.schuelerhilfe.de
/gute-noten
CODE 3034

bearbeitet am   zu erreichende Punktzahl: **12**   erreichte Punktzahl des Schülers

➡ Ab **10** erreichten Punkten kannst du zum nächsten Test übergehen.

Test 41 — Bedingungssätze – if-clauses Typ 1

Schwierigkeits-grad

A1 Entscheide, ob die Zeitformen der *if-clauses* korrekt verwendet wurden. [ ] 5

	richtig	falsch
a) If I hurry up, I will catch the train.	☐	☐
b) If the sun shines, we would meet in the park.	☐	☐
c) They can write a letter to him, if they find the pen.	☐	☐
d) If grandma was rich, she will give me some money.	☐	☐
e) Ann will know her mark, if she comes to class today.	☐	☐

A2 Kreuze die Verbform an, die in die Lücke muss. [ ] 5

a) If the children _____ kind, they will get presents on Christmas Eve.

☐ be   ☐ are   ☐ were   ☐ will be

b) If Moritz _____ carefully, he will get the answer.

☐ would listen   ☐ listens   ☐ listen   ☐ listened

c) If you _____ a witch in the forest, do not drink her magical drink!

☐ saw   ☐ would see   ☐ see   ☐ have seen

d) He will talk about his latest idea, if you _____ doctor Frankenstein.

☐ visited   ☐ would visit   ☐ visits   ☐ visit

e) An evil magician will lock you up, if you _____ into his eyes.

☐ look   ☐ had looked   ☐ will look   ☐ looked

A3 Beende die Hauptsätze der *if-clauses* mithilfe der angegebenen Wörter. [ ] 8

a) If I find her number, I _____ her. *(call)*

b) If Thomas does not go to school, he _____ his friends. *(not / meet)*

c) If it snows, Julie and Sarah _____ a ski course. *(do)*

d) My husband _____ my grandma, if I do not tell him to. *(not / phone)*

e) _____ out of the house, if you hear the fire alert! *(run)*

f) If somebody unknown knocks on the door, _____! *(not / open)*

g) If you fall into the pool, all people around _____. *(laugh)*

h) If you go to bed early, you _____ longer. *(can / sleep)*

oder:
www.schuelerhilfe.de
/gute-noten
CODE 3034

bearbeitet am [ ]   zu erreichende Punktzahl: 18   erreichte Punktzahl des Schülers [ ]

➡ Ab **14** erreichten Punkten kannst du zum nächsten Test übergehen.

© ZGS Bildungs-GmbH   Englisch 7/8 ▪ 47

Test 42   Bedingungssätze – if-clauses Typ 1

Schwierigkeits-grad

A 1 Entscheide, welche Konstruktionen zur Bildung der *if-clauses* richtig oder falsch sind.   5

		richtig	falsch
a)	*If* + Present Tense + will-future	☐	☐
b)	*If* + Present Tense + modal auxiliary + infinitive	☐	☐
c)	*If* + Past Tense + will-future	☐	☐
d)	*If* + Past Perfect + would + infinitive	☐	☐
e)	*If* + Present Tense + imperative	☐	☐

A 2 Die Sätze stellen Werbesprüche dar. Formuliere anhand der angegebenen Satzteile vollständige *if-clauses*.   4

Example

WHIRL washing powder / cleaner clothes ➡ If you use WHIRL washing powder, your clothes will be cleaner.

a) SPLASH bubble bath / feel like a new-born baby

   ....

b) SOFT shampoo / shiny hair

   ....

c) GENTLE soap / softer skin

   ....

d) WIZARD vacuum cleaner / spend less time on housework

   ....

A 3 Vervollständige die Sätze mithilfe der Verben in Klammern.   6

a) If dad .... *(buy)* me an ice-cream, I .... *(wash)* the dishes.

b) If my parents .... *(win)* a lot of money, we .... *(move)* to a bigger house.

c) The students .... *(can / understand)* Shakespeare, if the teacher .... *(explain)* the texts well.

d) If you .... *(be able to come)* to my party, you .... *(meet)* some of my best friends.

e) I .... *(ask)* for some advice, if I .... *(have)* problems.

f) If Kelly .... *(finish)* her studies this year, she .... *(get)* a good job in Tom's office.

oder:
www.schuelerhilfe.de
/gute-noten
CODE   3034

---

bearbeitet am   zu erreichende Punktzahl: 15   erreichte Punktzahl des Schülers

➡ Ab **12** erreichten Punkten kannst du zum nächsten Test übergehen.

Test 43 — Bedingungssätze – if-clauses Typ 1

Schwierigkeits-
grad

A1 Markiere den Hauptsatz. 7

a) If it rains, I will go home.

b) If she doesn't call me, I will be very sad.

c) I will be better in English, if I work harder.

d) If I work harder, I will get more money.

e) You will meet your friends, if you go to school.

f) If you visit me, we will eat cake.

g) I you do your homework after school, you can meet your friends.

A2 Füge *If* an der richtigen Stelle im Satz ein. 9

a) .... you play football, ... you will meet new friends.

b) .... the sun shines, ... we will drive to the beach.

c) .... My parents will be happy, ... I clean the kitchen.

d) .... Sandra doesn't feel good, ... her mother will bring her to the hospital.

e) .... We will spend our holiday in Spain, ... my mother earns enough money.

f) .... I will not go to school, ... it rains.

g) .... the weather is good, ... we will buy ice-cream.

h) .... she studies more, ... she will pass the test.

i) .... I run a lot, ... I will be very tired.

A3 Setze das Verb in der Klammer in der richtigen Zeitform ein. 10

a) If you .... *(be)* happy, I .... *(be)* happy, too.

b) If I .... *(learn)* a lot, I .... *(be)* good at school.

c) We .... *(leave)* early, if you .... *(do)* your homework as soon as possible.

d) I .... *(help)* you, if you .... *(need)* help.

e) If you .... *(leave)*, I .... *(follow)* you.

f) My friend .... *(visit)* me, if he .... *(have)* enough time.

g) I .... *(cook)* dinner, if you .... *(be)* home early.

h) If I .... *(go)* home early, my parents .... *(not be)* angry.

i) If the weather .... *(be)* good, we .... *(go)* to the zoo.

j) If she .... *(meet)* him, they .... *(eat)* lunch together.

oder:
www.schuelerhilfe.de
/gute-noten
CODE 3034

bearbeitet am .... zu erreichende Punktzahl: 26 erreichte Punktzahl des Schülers ....

➡ Ab **21** erreichten Punkten kannst du zum nächsten Test übergehen.

Test 44 **Bedingungssätze – if-clauses Typ 1**

Schwierigkeits-grad

A1 Füge die passenden Haupt- und Nebensätze zusammen. `10`

if I help my little sister · My legs will hurt · we will not have a barbecue outside · I will enjoy the sea ·
If we go to the restaurant · I will help you · I will be tired the next day · she will not get to know you ·
I will pick you up at 11 pm · If it snows

a) If you don't talk to her, ...

b) If it rains tomorrow, ...

c) My mother will be happy, ...

d) ...., I will be cold.

e) If I stay awake the whole night, ...

f) ...., if we have to run a lot.

g) If we drive to the beach, ...

h) ...., I will eat pizza.

i) If you go out tonight, ...

j) ...., if this exercise is too difficult.

A2 Wähle das richtige Verb aus und setze es in die Lücke ein. `10`

are · will see · is · will visit · will take · do · meet · will leave · will meet · will have · is ·
miss · visits · are · will be · takes · will spend · can ask · go · can take

a) If you .... your homework every day, you .... good at school.

b) If you .... at home at 12 o'clock, I .... you.

c) We .... her about the weekend, if we .... her.

d) She .... the Big Ben, if she .... London.

e) If I .... the bus, I .... a taxi.

f) If the weather .... good, we .... a pool party.

g) If we .... shopping, I .... a lot of money.

h) We .... early, if the movie .... not interesting.

i) We .... the train, if you .... on time.

j) We .... her, if she .... the same bus.

oder:
www.schuelerhilfe.de
/gute-noten
CODE `3034`

bearbeitet am _____   zu erreichende Punktzahl: 20   erreichte Punktzahl des Schülers _____

➡ Ab **16** erreichten Punkten kannst du zum nächsten Test übergehen.

© ZGS Bildungs-GmbH   Englisch 7/8 • 50

Test 45 — Bedingungssätze – if-clauses Typ 1

Schwierigkeitsgrad

A1 Erstelle aus den zwei gegebenen Sätzen *if-clauses Typ I.* | 6

a) You visit me. I am very happy. ....

b) I meet my friends. My mother needs no help. ....

c) We buy a new car. We have enough money. ....

d) My friend comes. We eat cake. ....

e) We get a cat. I take care of the cat. ....

f) We meet. We can have a dinner. ....

A2 In die Sätze haben sich Fehler eingeschlichen. Markiere die Fehler und korrigiere sie. | 6

a) I leave, if you are late. ....

b) If I will have enough money, I will buy a new car. ....

c) I will pass the test, if I studies more. ....

d) I will went to Australia, if I finish school. ....

e) If we stay at a hotel, Ibe very relaxed. ....

f) I will ask you, if I needed your help. ....

A3 Übersetze ins Englische. Verwende *if-clauses Typ I.* | 4

a) Wenn sie vorbeikommt, werden wir Tee trinken.

....

b) Wenn sie mich ignoriert, werde ich sehr traurig sein.

....

c) Wenn er pünktlich ist, bekommen wir den Zug.

....

d) Wenn du dein Zimmer aufräumst, wirst du deine Freunde besuchen.

....

oder:
www.schuelerhilfe.de
/gute-noten
CODE 3034

bearbeitet am   zu erreichende Punktzahl: 16   erreichte Punktzahl des Schülers

➡ Ab **13** erreichten Punkten kannst du zum nächsten Test übergehen.

Test 46 — Bedingungssätze – if-clauses Typ 2

Schwierigkeits-
grad

A1 **Kreuze alle Sätze an, die einen *if-clause Typ II* enthalten.** | 2 |

a) If I was you, I would hurry up. ☐

b) If you miss the train, your mom will not be very pleased. ☐

c) Would you have become a pilot if you had passed the test? ☐

d) You would be very happy if you won one million pounds. ☐

A2 **Vervollständige die *if-clauses* mit den Verben in Klammern. Nutze das *Simple Past.*** | 5 |

a) If I .... *(to have)* time on Saturday, I would go to the cinema.

b) If the teachers .... *(to decide)* to read the texts again, the pupils would have better chances.

c) She would participate in a party if they .... *(to realise)* their party program.

d) Would you visit the zoo of London if you .... *(to be)* there?

e) If grandpa .... *(to can)* drive a car, he would buy himself a Ferrari.

A3 **Verneine die Hauptsätze der *if-clauses.*** | 4 |

a) The cats would eat the birds on the tree if there was a dog in the garden.

....

b) If my family won one million euros, we would live in a castle.

....

c) If Jenny's husband was a soldier, she would be very happy.

....

d) Our school's athletes would win the contest even if they practiced more.

....

oder:
www.schuelerhilfe.de
/gute-noten
CODE 6937

bearbeitet am   **zu erreichende Punktzahl: 11**   **erreichte Punktzahl des Schülers**

➡ Ab **9** erreichten Punkten kannst du zum nächsten Test übergehen.

Test 47 — Bedingungssätze – if-clauses Typ 2

Schwierigkeitsgrad

A1 Entscheide, bei welchen der folgenden Sätze die Zeitformen des *if-clause Typ II* korrekt verwendet wurden.

2

a) If I saw the president of the USA, I would start arguing with him. ☐

b) If the pilots miss their train, the plane will start later. ☐

c) Would you buy a restaurant if you had enough money? ☐

d) You could have been very happy if you had bet with me. ☐

A2 Vervollständige die Hauptsätze der *if-clauses* mit den Verben in Klammern.

6

a) If Lucy learned more for the test, she .... *(not / to get)* a bad quote.

b) If I knew you were there, I .... *(to bake)* muffins.

c) .... you .... *(to eat)* fish if you lived at the coast?

d) When .... you .... *(to sleep)* if you worked as a baker?

e) If you were a police officer, you .... always .... *(to drive)* carefully.

f) If dad sang the song, he .... *(not / to be)* in the rhythm.

A3 Kreuze diejenige Verbform an, die anstelle der Lücke möglich ist.

4

a) If Susanna .... in the camp, she would become a sports teacher.

☐ is ☐ was ☐ have been

b) If the Millers .... the right door, they would win a car.

☐ would choose ☐ chose ☐ had chosen

c) If Tom said the truth, Linda .... him.

☐ had forgiven ☐ would forgive ☐ forgives

d) If my French teacher taught us vocabulary, we .... better.

☐ could speak ☐ can speak ☐ spoke

bearbeitet am .... zu erreichende Punktzahl: 12 erreichte Punktzahl des Schülers ....

➡ Ab **10** erreichten Punkten kannst du zum nächsten Test übergehen.

Test 48 — Bedingungssätze – if-clauses Typ 2

Schwierigkeits-
grad

A 1 Bilde aus beiden Sätzen einen einzigen Satz, indem du einen *if-clause Typ II* bildest. | 4

a) I would be famous.
I was a movie star in Hollywood.

....

b) My hamster would not be fat.
I gave him good food.

....

c) My friends wondered what could happen.
Someone kidnapped me in Brazil.

....

d) He stopped playing this dangerous sport.
He would still be healthy.

....

A 2 Kreuze an, wenn der Satz richtig gebildet wurde. Korrigiere Sätze, die falsch gebildet | 4
wurden.

a) He would get more attention, if he would not be scared of girls.   ☐

....

b) Denise could swim well, if she trained more often.   ☐

....

c) The boys would get good marks, if they do not talk all the time.   ☐

....

d) If my sister would get a cat, I want to have a snake   ☐

....

oder:
www.schuelerhilfe.de
/gute-noten
CODE 6937

bearbeitet am   **zu erreichende Punktzahl: 8**   **erreichte Punktzahl des Schülers**

➡ Ab **6** erreichten Punkten kannst du zum nächsten Test übergehen.

Test 49 — Bedingungssätze – if-clauses Typ 2

Schwierigkeits-
grad

A1 — Markiere den Hauptsatz.

7

a) If Sandra was home, she would prepare dinner.

b) I would travel around the world, if I had enough money.

c) If I were you, I would meet her.

d) If we lived far away, she would visit us.

e) I would see you, if I had more time.

f) If I was not ill, I would play football.

g) If you lived in Spain, I would visit you very often.

A2 — Füge *if* an der richtigen Stelle im Satz ein.

9

a) .... you were interested, ... you could meet her.

b) .... I would buy a new car, ... I were rich.

c) .... they liked tennis, ... we could play together.

d) .... you read more newspaper, ... you would be better informed.

e) .... you didn't lock your car, ... it would be stolen.

f) .... you would know it, ... you listened to me.

g) .... she would be better at school, ... she did her homework.

h) .... he exercised more, ... he would be fitter.

i) .... he left her, ... she would be sad.

A3 — Setze das Verb in der Klammer in der richtigen Zeitform ein. Ergänze wenn nötig *would, could* oder *might*.

10

a) If I .... *(be)* you, I .... *(listen)* to her.

b) If she .... *(have)* more time, she .... *(play)* soccer.

c) I .... *(buy)* me a car, if my parents .... *(have)* more money.

d) If you .... *(be)* home early, I .... *(order)* pizza.

e) If we .... *(be)* friends, we .... *(do)* everything together.

f) I .... *(go)* to school, if I .... *(be)* not ill.

g) We .... *(visit)* my grandmother, if we .... *(not live)* far away.

h) If she .... *(find)* a wallet, she .... *(bring)* it to the police.

i) If he .... *(not invite)* you, you .... *(be)* very angry.

j) If the computer .... *(not work)*, they .... *(not work)*.

oder:
www.schuelerhilfe.de
/gute-noten
CODE 6937

bearbeitet am .... zu erreichende Punktzahl: 26 erreichte Punktzahl des Schülers ....

➡ Ab **21** erreichten Punkten kannst du zum nächsten Test übergehen.

Schwierigkeits-
grad

A 1   Füge die passenden Haupt- und Nebensätze zusammen.   10

> I would save a lot of time · he would marry her · f I had a mobile phone · If my father knew this ·
> If we had more time · We could meet each other · I would go swimming with you ·
> She would help you · if it rained · if we were rich

a) ...., we would go on holiday.

b) If he loved her, ...

c) They would cancel the pool-party, ...

d) If you did my homework, ...

e) We would buy a big house, ...

f) ...., he would be very angry.

g) If I felt better, ...

h) ...., if you lived in Germany.

i) ...., I would be better connected to my friends.

j) ...., if you needed help.

A 2   Wähle das richtige Verb aus und setze es in die Lücke ein.   8

> lived · could get · had · would do · were · did · went · would invite · would buy · could buy ·
> met · won · would help · would go · would be · were

a) If you .... your homework, you .... better at school.

b) If we .... a lot of money, we .... a house in Miami.

c) I .... what I want, if I .... alone.

d) I .... you everything, if I .... the lottery.

e) If my parents .... rich, we .... a house cleaner.

f) If you .... to the teacher, he .... you.

g) If I .... you, I .... to the doctor.

h) If we .... each other, I .... you for a drink.

bearbeitet am   zu erreichende Punktzahl: 18   erreichte Punktzahl des Schülers

➡ Ab **14** erreichten Punkten kannst du zum nächsten Test übergehen.

LE 5: Satzgefüge – Nebensätze

Bedingungssätze – if-clauses Typ 2

Schwierigkeits-
grad

A 1 In die Sätze haben sich Fehler eingeschlichen. Markiere die Fehler und korrigiere sie. | 9

a) I would donate a lot, if I have enough money. ....

b) I would gave you a present, if I knew your birthday. ....

c) If I knew your address, I visit you. ....

d) If I have a watch, I would be on time. ....

e) If I was you, I will meet her. ....

f) If you were late, I would left. ....

g) You would knew her, if you were more often at school. ....

h) She would like you, if you was more friendly. ....

i) He were very happy, if you visited him. ....

A 2 Ordne die Aussagesätze richtig an und verwende den *if clause Typ II.* | 8
Achte dabei auf die richtigen Verbformen und Zeichensetzung. Starte mit dem Nebensatz.

a) taller · *(to)* be · I · basketball · *(to)* play · if · I

....

b) if · *(to)* earn · you · *(to)* work · more · money · you

....

c) money · if · *(to)* buy · new · *(to)* have · a · I · a · I · lot · of · bike

....

d) we · we · more · *(to)* talk · if · each · about · other · *(to)* know

....

e) bag · *(to)* be · *(to)* lose · I · very · sad · I · if · my

....

f) *(to)* pass · *(to)* study · if · I · exam · I · the

....

g) you · *(to)* call · *(to)* be · If · I · him · I

....

h) address · If · *(to)* write · I · his · *(to)* know · letter · a · him · I

....

oder:
www.schuelerhilfe.de
/gute-noten
CODE 6937

bearbeitet am [   ] zu erreichende Punktzahl: 17 erreichte Punktzahl des Schülers [   ]

➡ Ab **14** erreichten Punkten kannst du zum nächsten Test übergehen.

Test 52 — Bedingungssätze – if-clauses Typ 3

Schwierigkeits-
grad

A1 Kreuze diejenigen Sätze an, die im *if-clause type III* stehen. `2`

a) If I hurry up, I will catch my train. ☐

b) When you win the match, everyone will be happy. ☐

c) If I was a teacher, I would play a lot of games in my lessons. ☐

d) I would have won the lottery if I had bought a ticket. ☐

e) If I had had the chance, I would have climbed the Mount Everest. ☐

A2 Setze die Verbformen im *Past Perfect* ein, sodass ein korrekter *if-clause type III* entsteht. `4`

a) If the children .... *(to shout)* louder, the mother might have heard them.

b) We could have helped grandma if she .... *(to tell)* us about her problems.

c) What would have happened if I .... *(to become)* president of the United States of America?

d) If the headmaster .... *(call)* the parents yesterday, the pupils would not have gone to school this morning.

A3 Kreuze die richtige Verbform an, die den Hauptsatz vom *if-clause type III* ergänzen könnte. `3`

a) If I had not lost my purse, I .... new folders.

   ☐ could have bought   ☐ could buy

b) What .... if I had gone to university last year?

   ☐ would have happened   ☐ will happen

c) If Peter had decided to move earlier, he .... in a better flat.

   ☐ might have lived   ☐ would live

oder:
www.schuelerhilfe.de
/gute-noten
CODE 3262

bearbeitet am .... zu erreichende Punktzahl: 9 erreichte Punktzahl des Schülers ....

➡ Ab **7** erreichten Punkten kannst du zum nächsten Test übergehen.

© ZGS Bildungs-GmbH *Englisch 7/8* ▪ 58

Test 53   Bedingungssätze – if-clauses Typ 3

Schwierigkeits-
grad

A 1   **Kreuze denjenigen Satz an, der im _if-clause type III_ steht.**   1

a)   If I learned more vocabulary, I would get better marks in written tests.   □

b)   I might have become president of our chess club if I had won all matches.   □

c)   I can see my new dog coming home if I leave school immediately after class.   □

A 2   **Setze die Verbformen für die Hauptsätze so ein, dass ein korrekter _if-clause type III_ entsteht.**   4

a)   If the German teacher had been less ill, we .... _(to read)_ the whole novel.

b)   If Susan's husband had caught the ball, the window .... _(not / to break)_ into pieces.

c)   James .... _(to sing)_ in the choir if the music teacher had asked him.

d)   If my parents had not phoned Lisa, they .... _(not/ to know)_ about the party.

A 3   **Verneine die Hauptsätze und Nebensätze der folgenden _if-clauses type III_.**   4

a)   If I had lost my bag, I would have called the police.

....

b)   The president would have given a speech if he had been ill.

....

oder:
www.schuelerhilfe.de
/gute-noten
CODE   3262

---

bearbeitet am   **zu erreichende Punktzahl: 9**   **erreichte Punktzahl des Schülers**

➡ **Ab 7 erreichten Punkten kannst du zum nächsten Test übergehen.**

Test 54   Bedingungssätze – if-clauses Typ 3

Schwierigkeits-grad

A1   Kreuze alle Aussagen zu den *if-clauses type III* an, die zutreffend sind.   `3`

a)   The tense of the if-clause type III is the Past Perfect.   ☐

b)   In the main clause there is more than one possibility of the auxiliary verb.   ☐

c)   The tense of the main clause is called conditional I.   ☐

d)   If-clauses type III are so called "unreal" conditions.   ☐

A2   Vervollständige den Text mit den richtigen Verbformen. Achte auf die richtige Zeitform.   `12`

a)   On Tuesday I failed my German studies test. If I .... *(to do)* more work the night before,
I .... *(pass)* it.

b)   If I .... *(not / to go)* to the football game on Monday night, I ....
(not / to feel) so tired on Tuesday.

c)   On Wednesday grandpa forgot to pick me up from football practice. If I .... *(to phone)*
him, he .... *(not / to forget)* to pick me up.

d)   On Thursday I got in trouble in Biology, because I broke my model of a human brain during break.
If I .... *(not / to jump)* down the stairs, my model .... *(not / to fall)*
down. If I .... *(to have)* the model in the lesson, the teacher ....
(to give) me a great mark.

e)   On Saturday I got home really late, therefore my sister was mad, because we wanted to watch a movie.
If I .... *(to tell)* her that I was coming home late, she .... *(not / to be)*
mad and she .... *(not / to wait)* so long.

f)   On Sunday I left a notice in the pocket of my jeans. Mom washed them and the paper got wet.
If I .... *(to take)* the notice out, it .... *(not / to be)* wet.

A3   Entscheide, ob *might, would* oder *could* am besten in die Lücke passt.   `3`

a)   If the students had practised harder for the competition, they .... have been faster.

b)   If our school team had not been so slow, they .... have caught the others.

c)   If the weather conditions had not been so bad, they .... have had a
better chance.

oder:
www.schuelerhilfe.de
/gute-noten
CODE   3262

---

bearbeitet am ....   zu erreichende Punktzahl: 18   erreichte Punktzahl des Schülers ....

➡ Ab **14** erreichten Punkten kannst du zum nächsten Test übergehen.

Test 55 — Bedingungssätze – if-clauses Typ 3

Schwierigkeits-
grad

A1 Notiere, ob es sich um *if-clause Typ 1, 2* oder *3* handelt. | 7 |

a) If I had studied more, I would have passed the test.

b) If the weather is good, we will drive to the beach.

c) I would have been happy, if he had called me.

d) If you needed help, the teacher would help you.

e) If I had prepared the dinner, my parents would have been happy.

f) My teacher wouldn't have been angry, if I had done my homework.

g) If I had played guitar, I would not have been so unmusical.

A2 Füge *if* an der richtigen Stelle im Satz ein. | 7 |

a) .... I had known you, ... we would have been friends.

b) .... She would have been better in school, ... she had studied more.

c) .... you had visited her more often, ... she would not have forgotten you.

d) .... you had earned more money, ... you would have spent more time on vacation.

e) .... They would have been friendlier, ... you had not been so angry.

f) .... he had exercised, ... the team would have won the match.

g) .... He would not have been fat, ... he had not eaten so much.

A3 Setze das Verb in der Klammer in der richtigen Zeitform ein. Verwende *if-clauses Type III.* | 6 |

a) If we .... *(leave)* early, we .... *(get)* the train.

b) They .... *(be)* in love, if they .... *(meet)* each other.

c) If the weather .... *(be)* good, we .... *(go)* to the zoo.

d) If I .... *(be)* late at home, my parents .... *(be)* angry.

e) I .... *(get)* a lot of presents, if my birthday .... *(be)* yesterday.

f) You .... *(have)* more friends, if you .... *(be)* friendlier.

oder:
www.schuelerhilfe.de
/gute-noten
CODE   3262

---

bearbeitet am ....   zu erreichende Punktzahl: 20   erreichte Punktzahl des Schülers ....

➡ Ab **16** erreichten Punkten kannst du zum nächsten Test übergehen.

Test 56 — Bedingungssätze – if-clauses Typ 3

Schwierigkeits-grad

A1 Füge die passenden Haupt- und Nebensätze zusammen. | 10

> if I had had more money · if your house had been cleaner · If she had learned more ·
> If I had had more time · if his mobile phone had not been broken · I would have bought you a present ·
> They would have been earlier · I would not have eaten the pizza · She would have gone to work ·
> he would not have left her

a) If I had not been hungry, ...

b) I would have traveled a lot, ...

c) .... , I would have visited you.

d) .... , if she had not been ill.

e) He would have called you, ...

f) You would have found your keys, ...

g) .... , she would have passed the test.

h) If she had spent more time with him, ...

i) .... , if they had not sat in traffic.

j) If I had had more money, ...

A2 Wähle das richtige Verb aus und setze es in die passende Lücke ein. | 10

> would have opened · had had · would have seen · would have known · had had ·
> had not been · had not hurt · had not eaten · would have known · had visited · would have been ·
> had known · had talked · had bought · would not have taken · would have taken · would have baked ·
> would have done · would have had · had had

a) If we .... Berlin, we .... the Brandenburger Tor.

b) I .... the door, if I .... my keys.

c) I .... a cake, if I .... the recipe.

d) If they .... a car, they .... the bus.

e) If they .... more, they .... each other better.

f) You .... more words, if you .... a dictionary.

g) He .... more sports, if he .... his leg.

h) If her camera .... broken, she .... pictures.

i) He .... a better general education, if

he .... more money.

j) He .... hungry, if he .... the
whole cake.

oder:
www.schuelerhilfe.de
/gute-noten
CODE 3262

bearbeitet am .... zu erreichende Punktzahl: 20 erreichte Punktzahl des Schülers ....

➡ Ab **16** erreichten Punkten kannst du zum nächsten Test übergehen.

Test 57 — **Bedingungssätze – if-clauses Typ 3**

Schwierigkeitsgrad

A1 Ergänze das fehlende Wort. | 6

a) If I .... studied more, I would .... understood the question.

b) If we had got a cat, I would have .... care of it.

c) We .... have had a dinner, if we .... met.

d) If we had .... enough money, we would have bought a new car.

e) We would have done sports, ... we had had less school.

f) If I had had a mobile phone, I would .... called you.

A2 In die Sätze haben sich Fehler eingeschlichen. Markiere die Fehler und korrigiere sie. | 6

a) If we have learned more, we would have passed the test.

b) If we had talked about the problem, we have found a solution.

c) I would have buy you a present, if we had been friends.

d) I would have visited my friend, if he has lived next to me.

e) If I had work more, I would have had more money.

f) I would have helped you, if you asked me.

A3 Ordne die Sätze richtig an und verwende *if-clauses Typ III*. Achte auf die richtige Form der Verben und auf die Zeichensetzung. Starte mit dem Nebensatz. | 5

a) me · if · *(to)* be · good · *(to)* visit · she · we · friends

b) *(to)* do · her · she · mother · excercises · if · angry · not · her · *(to)* be

c) If · *(to)* get · *(to)* get · up · the · we · earlier · train · we

d) if · he · *(to)* have · friendly · friends · *(to)* be · more · he

e) money · *(to)* buy · car · *(to)* save · he · he · a · if

oder:
www.schuelerhilfe.de
/gute-noten
CODE 3262

bearbeitet am _____   zu erreichende Punktzahl: 17   erreichte Punktzahl des Schülers _____

➡ Ab **14** erreichten Punkten kannst du zum nächsten Test übergehen.

© ZGS Bildungs-GmbH

Englisch 7/8 • 63

Test 58 · Relativsätze – relative clauses mit *who, which* oder *that*

Schwierigkeits-grad

A1 Kreuze alle Sätze an, die einen Relativsatz enthalten. `3`

a) The boy who delivered the newspapers has moved away. ☐

b) Who has delivered the newspapers? ☐

c) Take the videos that are on the table. ☐

d) It's a problem that the videos are on the table. ☐

e) She wants a pet which is cuddy. ☐

f) Which pet do you like? ☐

A2 Kreuze an, ob die folgenden Aussagen richtig oder falsch sind. `4`

	richtig	falsch
a) *Who* is a question word only.	☐	☐
b) The relative pronoun *that* is used with both persons and things.	☐	☐
c) With things and animals we use *which* or *that*.	☐	☐
d) With people we use *who* or *that*.	☐	☐

A3 Entscheide dich für *who* oder *which*. `7`

a) The man .... phoned us earlier is here now.

b) I really like the cat .... we saw at grandma's house.

c) Here are some photos .... show my family.

d) Can you please ask the man .... we talked to last week?

e) The people .... we met at the concert were nice.

f) I need someone .... could help me in the garden.

g) The books .... I've written are all for my girlfriend.

bearbeitet am .... zu erreichende Punktzahl: 14 erreichte Punktzahl des Schülers ....

➡ Ab **11** erreichten Punkten kannst du zum nächsten Test übergehen.

Test 59 — Relativsätze – relative clauses mit *who, which* oder *that*

Schwierigkeits-
grad

A1 Kreuze alle möglichen Relativpronomen an, die die Lücke ersetzen können. | 8

a) The woman .... is waiting at the bus stop is my mom.

  ☐ that   ☐ who   ☐ which

b) Do you know the cat .... is climbing the tree over there?

  ☐ who   ☐ which   ☐ that

c) Was the book .... is sold in this shop written by you?

  ☐ which   ☐ that   ☐ who

d) I really like the pancakes .... are made by my grandmother.

  ☐ who   ☐ that   ☐ which

A2 Entscheide, ob die folgenden Sätze richtig oder falsch sind. | 5

	richtig	falsch
a) If you know the man which is looking at us please tell me.	☐	☐
b) I knew a dog who could bring the newspapers.	☐	☐
c) I will buy a magazine that is about horses.	☐	☐
d) You can ask the lady who told us the way last week for help.	☐	☐
e) In my opinion, the book which we read in class last lesson was very interesting.	☐	☐

A3 Setze das richtige Relativpronomen ein. | 6

a) Have you already done the homework .... our German teacher gave us?

b) My parents visited the city .... is the capital of Germany.

c) I don't like the teachers .... always let us write essays.

d) Julie says that woman .... works in the bakery makes the best cakes in the world.

e) If you see the police officer .... was standing near the traffic lights yesterday, please ask him your question concerning traffic law.

f) California is the state in .... one can find the Golden Gate Bridge.

oder:
www.schuelerhilfe.de
/gute-noten
CODE 6725

bearbeitet am .... zu erreichende Punktzahl: 19 erreichte Punktzahl des Schülers ....

➡ Ab **15** erreichten Punkten kannst du zum nächsten Test übergehen.

Test 60 — Relativsätze – relative clauses mit *who, which* oder *that*

Schwierigkeits-
grad

A 1 Entscheide, ob *who* oder *which* eingesetzt werden muss. | 7 |

a) Can you give me the new book .... I bought yesterday?

b) Was it Peter .... has just called?

c) What's the name of the song .... we were talking about for hours yesterday?

d) Have you talked to the man .... your parents introduced the day before?

e) I would kill for the sweets .... my grandma brought from Switzerland.

f) I know an actor .... has played in 1000 movies so far.

g) Please pass me the scarf .... is laying next to your chair.

A 2 Entscheide, ob die folgenden Sätze richtig oder falsch sind. | 4 |

	richtig	falsch
a) This is the soccer player that I told you about.	☐	☐
b) This is the soccer player about who I told you.	☐	☐
c) Here's the CD for that you've been looking.	☐	☐
d) Here's the CD which you've been looking for.	☐	☐

A 3 Vervollständige die angefangenen Definitionen mit einem Relativsatz. Nutze die gegebenen Stichworte und füge selbstständig *who, which* oder *that* ein. | 4 |

a) Palm trees are trees ....

in / often / the Caribbean / grow.

b) The Statue of Liberty is a sight ....

by / was given / France / to / the USA.

c) A headmaster is a person ....

works / in / a school.

d) A bed is a kind of furniture ....

people / sleep/ in.

oder:
www.schuelerhilfe.de
/gute-noten
CODE 6725

bearbeitet am .... zu erreichende Punktzahl: 15 erreichte Punktzahl des Schülers ....

➡ Ab **12** erreichten Punkten kannst du zum nächsten Test übergehen.

Test **61** Relativsätze – relative clauses mit *who, which* oder *that*

Schwierigkeits-
grad

A1 Entscheide bei welchen Sätzen es sich um Relativsätze handelt und kreuze diese an. | 7

a) Who broke the bottle? ☐

b) Is this the boy who hit you? ☐

c) I mean the tree that is in our backyard. ☐

d) Which one is your t-shirt, the black or the white one? ☐

e) This is the clock which was stolen two years ago. ☐

f) The girl who is crying is my younger sister. ☐

g) This is the dog that came into my house. ☐

h) The candle, which smells like vanilla, is the white one. ☐

i) That is my favourite book. ☐

j) Mia ist the girl who fell in love with my brother. ☐

A2 In einigen Sätzen haben sich Fehler bei den Relativpronomen eingeschlichen. | 5
Kreuze die richtigen Sätze an.

a) This ist the book which I read last week. ☐

b) This is my classmate which had a broken leg. ☐

c) My brother asked me if Caro was the girl who tried to call him. ☐

d) Budgies are animals which are able to fly. ☐

e) I don't like the boy that wrote the letter. ☐

f) Titanic was the last movie who I saw in the cinema. ☐

g) I'm going to buy a car which is cheaper than my old one. ☐

oder:
www.schuelerhilfe.de
/gute-noten
CODE 6725

bearbeitet am | **zu erreichende Punktzahl: 12** | **erreichte Punktzahl des Schülers**

➡ Ab **10** erreichten Punkten kannst du zum nächsten Test übergehen.

Test 62 — Relativsätze – relative clauses mit *who, which* oder *that*

Schwierigkeits-
grad

A 1   **Welche Aussagen sind richtig und welche falsch? Kreuze an.**   5

		richtig	falsch
a)	Relativsätze verwendet man, um eine Sache oder Person näher zu beschreiben, ohne einen zweiten Satz anzuhängen.	☐	☐
b)	*That* kann ausschließlich das Relativpronomen *which* ersetzen.	☐	☐
c)	Durch die Verwendung von Relativpronomen werden Wiederholungen vermieden.	☐	☐
d)	Das Relativpronomen *who* wird bei Tieren und Personen verwendet.	☐	☐
e)	Das Relativpronomen *which* wird bei Dingen und Gegenständen verwendet.	☐	☐

A 2   **Ergänze die Sätze mit den Relativpronomen *who* oder *which*.**   13

a)   This is the flower _____ has the most beautiful smell.

b)   I called the person _____ wanted to speak with me.

c)   Paul is the turtle _____ wants to bite all the other pets.

d)   The bakery _____ sells the best donuts is around the corner.

e)   Do you know the man _____ is talking to my wife?

f)   Janina is the girl _____ is the best tennis player in town.

g)   The animal _____ lives in Africa is a lion.

h)   The Millers are our new neighbours _____ live in the white house next door.

i)   People _____ live in China are Chinese.

j)   My friend _____ would like to take photos on my wedding is Andrea.

k)   "The Star" is the restaurant _____ belongs to my sister in law.

l)   Yvonne is the 35-year-old lady _____ protects animals.

m)   Ben is the man _____ flew to Poland last night.

oder:
www.schuelerhilfe.de
/gute-noten
CODE   6725

bearbeitet am   **zu erreichende Punktzahl: 18**   **erreichte Punktzahl des Schülers**

➡ Ab **14** erreichten Punkten kannst du zum nächsten Test übergehen.

LE 5: Satzgefüge – Nebensätze

Test 63 — Relativsätze – relative clauses mit *who*, *which* oder *that*

Schwierigkeits-grad

A 1 Forme die jeweils zwei Sätze in einen Relativsatz um. Verwende die Relativpronomen *who* und *which*.

`5`

a) A fir is a tree. A fir is used as a christmas tree in December.

....

b) This parakeet is a male. The parakeet has a blue nose.

....

c) Maja is a woman. Maja likes to read.

....

d) This is my new computer. I bought my new computer last Saturday.

....

e) Donald Trump is America's president. Donald Trump is criticized all over the world.

....

A 2 Bilde Relativsätze aus den vorgegebenen Wörtern. Verwende die Relativpronomen *who* und *which*.

`6`

a) I / paint/ my / have / to / house / red / has / window frames

....

b) the / I / jeans / I / yesterday / bought / like /

....

c) He / the / is / stole / my / heart / man / nine / ago / years

....

d) I / my / lost / voice / is / very / strong

....

e) this / man / wants / Is / the / to / you / marry

.... ?

f) are / do / eat / not / Vegans / animal / people / products

....

oder:
www.schuelerhilfe.de
/gute-noten
CODE 6725

---

bearbeitet am [   ]   zu erreichende Punktzahl: 11   erreichte Punktzahl des Schülers [   ]

➡ Ab **9** erreichten Punkten kannst du zum nächsten Test übergehen.

Test 64   Relativsätze – relative clauses mit *who, whose, who's* oder *whom*

Schwierigkeits-
grad

A1   Setze *who* oder *whose* in die passenden Lücken ein.   7

a)   She has a friend .... is called Amy.

b)   The girl .... twin sister is in my class speaks Chinese.

c)   The policeman .... caught the thief was nervous.

d)   He is the guy .... feeds our cat.

e)   I buy my eggs from a farmer .... chicken roam free.

f)   I saw a woman .... I thought was your mother.

g)   .... baby is this?

A2   Schreibe die Sätze so um, dass zwei Sätze entstehen.   6

a)   I know a girl whose favourite sport is tennis.

....

b)   This is the woman who had an accident.

....

c)   This is the first time we see that man who's smoking a cigarette.

....

d)   Do you like that boy whose favourite animals are dogs?

....

e)   This is the boy whose car is very fast.

....

f)   She is the one from whom I got the books.

....

oder:
www.schuelerhilfe.de
/gute-noten
CODE   6185

bearbeitet am ....   **zu erreichende Punktzahl: 13**   **erreichte Punktzahl des Schülers** ....

➡ Ab **10** erreichten Punkten kannst du zum nächsten Test übergehen.

Test 65 Relativsätze – relative clauses mit *who, whose, who's* oder *whom*

Schwierigkeits-grad

A1 **Verbinde die Sätze mit Hilfe der Relativpronomen.**   5

a) This is the girl. She helped me with my homework.

....

b) This is the boy. He studied maths with me.

....

c) This is my neighbour. His mother died.

....

d) This is a big city. Its name is Munich.

....

e) This is my friend. I gave my laptop to him.

....

A2 **Bringe die Satzteile in die richtige Reihenfolge.**   6

a) man / this / baked / cake / the / for / us / is / who

....

b) England / country / a / is / whose / inhabitants / speak / English

....

c) a / is / a / policeman / person / catches / who / thieves

....

d) someone / pilot / is / a / fly / able to / who's / planes

....

e) have / a / you / baby / crying / whole / day / the / who's

....

f) is / who / doctor / a / person / can / other / help / a / people

....

A3 **Fülle die Lücken mit dem richtigen Relativpronomen.**   5

a) Jan, ... my cousin, goes to Kindergarten.

b) I help my grandma .... leg is broken.

c) I can see someone .... in your house.

d) The girl .... buying presents is Lina.

e) I need someone .... can solve this exercise for me.

oder:
www.schuelerhilfe.de
/gute-noten
CODE 6185

---

bearbeitet am ⬚ **zu erreichende Punktzahl: 16** **erreichte Punktzahl des Schülers** ⬚

➡ **Ab 13** erreichten Punkten kannst du zum nächsten Test übergehen.

Test 66 — Relativsätze – relative clauses mit *who*, *whose*, *who's* oder *whom*

Schwierigkeits-
grad

A1 Trage das richtige Relativpronomen in die Lücke ein. Wähle zwischen *who, whose, who's* oder *whom.*　　　　　7

a) .... is he?

b) Once upon a time there was a girl .... name was Cinderella.

c) Do you know .... they are?

d) There is a woman .... staying here with us.

e) My parents from .... I borrowed some money are angry.

f) This is my grandpa .... always taking photos.

g) Do you know the author .... wrote this book?

A2 Übersetze ins Englische.　　　　　6

a) Ich habe eine E-Mail an meinen Papa gesendet, der in Amerika lebt.

....

b) Ich habe einen Freund, der seine Katze mit Käse füttert.

....

c) Das Mädchen, das neben mir wohnt, ist immer spät.

....

d) Kennst du diesen Typ, der gerade an der Bushaltestelle wartet.

....

e) Wir haben eine Großmutter, deren Eltern aus Russland kommen.

....

f) Habe ich dir nicht den Namen der Person gesagt, an die ich die Email gesendet habe?

....

oder:
www.schuelerhilfe.de
/gute-noten
CODE 6185

bearbeitet am 　　　　　　**zu erreichende Punktzahl: 13**　　　　**erreichte Punktzahl des Schülers**

➡ Ab **10** erreichten Punkten kannst du zum nächsten Test übergehen.

Test 67   Relativsätze – relative clauses mit *who, whose, who's* oder *whom*

Schwierigkeits-grad

A1   **Entscheide, ob die Aussagen richtig oder falsch sind.**   6

		richtig	falsch
a)	*Who's* steht für "who is".	☐	☐
b)	*Whose* ist die Vergangenheitsform von **who**.	☐	☐
c)	*Who* ist das Relativpronomen, welches sich auf Personen bezieht.	☐	☐
d)	*Whom* wird als Objekt für Personen verwendet.	☐	☐
e)	*Whose* steht als Zugehörigkeit für Personen, Tiere und Dinge.	☐	☐
f)	*Who* kann nicht durch **that** ersetzt werden.	☐	☐

A2   **Ergänze die Sätze mit *who* oder *whose*.**   12

a) Linda is the girl .... cat got kitten.

b) Andrew is the one .... likes to play football.

c) Mrs. O'Connor is the teacher .... teaches sports and history.

d) Ella is the mother .... daughter lives in America.

e) I'm going to call my sister .... owns a travel agency.

f) Do you see the man .... is wearing the white t-shirt?

g) This is Yvonne .... pets are pretty crazy.

h) This is Emilia .... husband is mostly working abroad.

i) My friend Janina, ... won 10 000 €, went to New York.

j) Andrea is the woman .... is always in a good mood.

k) The man .... job is to create good advertisements is my brother.

l) My mum, ... likes to read, is preparing lunch.

oder:
www.schuelerhilfe.de
/gute-noten
CODE   6185

bearbeitet am   zu erreichende Punktzahl: 18   erreichte Punktzahl des Schülers

➡ Ab **14** erreichten Punkten kannst du zum nächsten Test übergehen.

© ZGS Bildungs-GmbH   *Englisch 7/8* • 73

Test 68 — Relativsätze – relative clauses mit *who, whose, who's* oder *whom*

Schwierigkeits-
grad

A1 Ergänze die Sätze, indem du *who, whose* oder *who's* einfügst. 8

a) Emma is the lady .... quite busy all day.

b) .... is your oldest brother?

c) Andrew is the man .... house is always clean.

d) My husband, ... also works on weekends, wants to spend the next vacation in the USA.

e) I'm not that kind of person .... likes action movies.

f) The black car .... owner is the friendly man has been stolen.

g) My brother, ... a good singer, doesn't like to talk.

h) My father, ... birthday is next week, works in the Netherlands.

A2 Stelle die Sätze und Fragen in die richtige Reihenfolge. 6

a) the / Who's / football / best / in / the / world / player

.... ?

b) is / the / Elliot / man / broke / my / who / heart

....

c) Magdalena / the / is / whose / to / woman / children / like / swim

....

d) did / cookies / you / bake / the / whom / For

.... ?

e) whom / the / go / To / Millers / did

.... ?

f) may / To / concern / this / whom

....

oder:
www.schuelerhilfe.de
/gute-noten
CODE 6185

bearbeitet am [   ]   zu erreichende Punktzahl: 14   erreichte Punktzahl des Schülers [   ]

➤ Ab **11** erreichten Punkten kannst du zum nächsten Test übergehen.

Test 69 — Relativsätze – relative clauses mit *who, whose, who's* oder *whom*

Schwierigkeits-grad

A 1 **Erstelle aus den jeweils beiden Sätzen einen Satz. Verbinde sie mit den Relativpronomen** *who, whose, who's* **oder** *whom.* `7`

a) My sister is happy. She is pregnant.

....

b) This is my friend Naomi. She will bring us to the airport.

....

c) This is my aunt. She's singing all day.

....

d) This is the old lady. Her name is Sophia.

....

e) The old man died. I sold my house to the old man.

....

f) May I introduce you to my little sister? My little sister was born in 2010.

....

g) This is Kai. He's the love of my life.

....

A 2 **In einigen der folgenden Sätze haben sich Fehler eingeschlichen.** `5`
Entscheide, welche richtig oder falsch sind.

		richtig	falsch
a)	This is Sally who's the oldest of three girls.	☐	☐
b)	This is Bernd who's dog is 15 years old.	☐	☐
c)	Maja ist he daughter whom is the best doing sports.	☐	☐
d)	This is Selma whose dog sleeps on the sofa all night long.	☐	☐
e)	My brother who likes to play football broke his leg.	☐	☐

oder:
www.schuelerhilfe.de
/gute-noten
CODE `6185`

bearbeitet am [   ]   **zu erreichende Punktzahl: 12**   **erreichte Punktzahl des Schülers** [   ]

➡ Ab **10** erreichten Punkten kannst du zum nächsten Test übergehen.

Test **70** Relativsätze ohne Relativpronomen – contact clauses

Schwierigkeits-grad

A1 **Kreuze alle Sätze an, die richtig sind.**   `10`

a) Sandra is the girl who is standing next to Tim. ☐
Sandra is the girl is standing next to Tim. ☐
Sandra is the girl which is standing next to Tim. ☐

b) This is the boy which I met yesterday. ☐
This is the boy I met yesterday. ☐
This is the boy who I met yesterday. ☐

c) Have you seen my car which was parked next to the tree? ☐
Have you seen my car who was parked next to the tree? ☐
Have you seen my car was parked next to the tree? ☐

d) That's the girl who lives in Germany. ☐
That's the girl lives in Germany. ☐
That's the girl this lives in Germany. ☐

e) We met someone which was very tall. ☐
We met someone who was very tall. ☐
We met someone was very tall. ☐

f) The man you see in the red car is my dad. ☐
The man who you see in the red car is my dad. ☐
The man whose you see in the red car is my dad. ☐

g) The summer is the time of the year when it is warm outside. ☐
The summer is the time of the year it is warm outside. ☐
The summer is the time of the year than it is warm outside. ☐

A2 **Forme die *contact clauses* in Relativsätze um.**   `6`

a) This was an interesting book I read last week.

....

b) Do you like Anna I met in High School?

....

c) This is the new mobile phone I bought yesterday.

....

d) That's the boy I remember well.

....

e) Do you see the girl he's talking to?

....

f) This is the book I got as a present.

....

oder:
www.schuelerhilfe.de
/gute-noten
CODE `8415`

bearbeitet am .... zu erreichende Punktzahl: **16** erreichte Punktzahl des Schülers

➡ Ab **13** erreichten Punkten kannst du zum nächsten Test übergehen.

Test 71 Relativsätze ohne Relativpronomen – contact clauses

Schwierigkeits-grad

A1 Bilde aus den Relativsätzen bzw. aus den zwei Sätzen *contact clauses.* 7

a) Sam is the boy who I met yesterday.

....

b) This is the dog. My parents gave this dog to me on my last birthday.

....

c) This is my new car which I bought last week.

....

d) I remember the article. You told me about it.

....

e) These are my parents. I picked them up at the airport.

....

f) The woman who you see across the street is my mother.

....

g) Have you seen the people that we met last weekend?

....

A2 In manchen der folgenden Sätze haben sich Fehler eingeschlichen. Korrigiere die 8
fehlerhaften Sätze und markiere die richtigen Sätze mit einem Kreuz.

a) The dog is playing with the ball is mine.

....

b) Tom is the boy plays football.

....

c) Listen to the woman is wearing the red pullover.

....

d) Who was the girl you were sitting next to?

....

e) Look at the boys who are playing football.

....

f) Anna is the girl plays guitar.

....

g) Listen to the poem she is reading.

....

h) This is the boy lost his keys.

....

oder:
www.schuelerhilfe.de
/gute-noten
CODE 8415

bearbeitet am _____   zu erreichende Punktzahl: 15   erreichte Punktzahl des Schülers _____

➡ Ab **12** erreichten Punkten kannst du zum nächsten Test übergehen.

Test 72   Relativsätze ohne Relativpronomen – contact clauses

Schwierigkeits-
grad

A1   **Fülle die Lücken mit einem passenden Relativpronomen. Lasse die Lücke leer, wenn ein *contact clause* möglich ist.**   10

a)   Listen to the music .... Lisa is playing with her guitar.

b)   We met Sam .... lives in Berlin.

c)   A zoo is a place .... you can see a lot of animals.

d)   My mother has a dog .... has brown fur.

e)   This is the girl .... friend lives in Canada.

f)   This is Tom .... you met yesterday.

g)   Sam is the man .... has played tennis since 2012.

h)   Look at the picture .... Anna is painting.

i)   The cat .... sits under the table is mine.

j)   This was my sister .... we met last night.

A2   **Übersetze ins Englische. Verwende *contact clauses* wenn möglich.**   9

a)   Anna ist das Mädchen, das wir gestern getroffen haben.

....

b)   Das ist mein Hund, der draußen im Garten ist.

....

c)   Das sind die Jungs, die ich gestern gesehen habe.

....

d)   Hier sind deine Schlüssel, die du vor zwei Tagen verloren hast.

....

e)   Das ist das Mädchen, dessen Vater in einem Krankenhaus arbeitet.

....

f)   Schau dir das niedliche Kaninchen an, welches ich als Geschenk bekommen habe.

....

g)   Hör der Frau zu, die einen roten Pullover trägt.

....

h)   Das war meine Schwester, die gestern im Café war.

....

i)   Das ist das Mädchen, das nach England reist.

....

oder:
www.schuelerhilfe.de
/gute-noten
CODE   8415

bearbeitet am   **zu erreichende Punktzahl: 19**   **erreichte Punktzahl des Schülers**

➡ Ab **15** erreichten Punkten kannst du zum nächsten Test übergehen.

Test 73 Relativsätze ohne Relativpronomen – contact clauses

Schwierigkeits-
grad

A1 **Kreuze die Sätze an, bei denen auf das Relativpronomen verzichtet werden kann.**   5

a) This is the window which I cleaned yesterday.   ☐

b) This is my mum who works in the bakery next door.   ☐

c) The man who is painting the wall is my husband.   ☐

d) Is this your friend who used to go to work by helicopter?   ☐

e) My dog, which is sitting in the garden, likes to play with a ball.   ☐

f) Have you seen my daughter who played in the garden?   ☐

g) This is the bike which I bought in June.   ☐

h) Do you like the dress that your mum bought for you?   ☐

i) This is the necklace that I wanted for my birthday.   ☐

j) You are the man that I've been looking for.   ☐

k) I'm looking for someone who is a good singer.   ☐

A2 **Schreibe die in Aufgabe 1 ausgewählten Sätze _ohne_ Relativpronomen auf.**   5

a) ....

b) ....

c) ....

d) ....

e) ....

oder:
www.schuelerhilfe.de
/gute-noten
CODE   8415

bearbeitet am   **zu erreichende Punktzahl: 10**   **erreichte Punktzahl des Schülers**

➡ Ab **8** erreichten Punkten kannst du zum nächsten Test übergehen.

Test 74 — Relativsätze ohne Relativpronomen – contact clauses

Schwierigkeits-
grad

A1 **Forme die Sätze in jeweils einen Satz um. Verzichte auf das Relativpronomen.** 6

a) I read a book. The book has 1000 pages.

The book ....

b) Last night I listened to my favourite song. The song was a hit in 1995.

My favourite song ....

c) The cat is sleeping in my bed. I love the cat so much.

The cat ....

d) I'm watching a thriller at the moment. It is very exciting.

The thriller ....

e) Anna wore a beautiful golden ring last night. Did you see it?

Did you see ....

f) I bought a new jacket for my son. Do you like it?

Do you like ....

A2 **In einigen Sätzen haben sich Fehler eingeschlichen. Finde diese und schreibe den Satz korrekt auf.** 6

a) The boy is looking at you is Paul.

....

b) The dog that is barking wants to play.

....

c) The mobile phone I got is a Samsung.

....

d) My friend I called yesterday lives in China.

....

e) The baby is crying is my cousin.

....

f) The reason I'm calling is to say that I miss you.

....

oder:
www.schuelerhilfe.de
/gute-noten
CODE 8415

bearbeitet am .... **zu erreichende Punktzahl: 12** **erreichte Punktzahl des Schülers** ....

➥ Ab **10** erreichten Punkten kannst du zum nächsten Test übergehen.

Test 75 Relativsätze ohne Relativpronomen – contact clauses

Schwierigkeits-
grad

A 1 Ergänze die Lücken mit den passenden Relativpronomen *(who/who's/which/whose)*. | 12
Wenn ein *contact clause* möglich ist, lass die Lücke leer.

a) Look at the picture .... Mary has drawn.

b) This is Matt .... dog likes to swim.

c) Yvonne .... 35 years old likes to sing.

d) Nica .... is a green bird likes to play with her mate called Joe.

e) Do you like the song .... they are singing?

f) I'm afraid of thunderstorms .... are very strong.

g) I'm that woman .... wants to move to the USA.

h) This is the flower .... smells like summer.

i) A lion is an animal .... mane is quite rough.

j) The place .... I want to live in is Boston.

k) The pullover .... I'm wearing is quite warm.

l) The car .... owner is my grandma is a SUV.

A 2 Beantworte die Fragen und verzichte wenn möglich auf das Relativpronomen. | 5

a) Q: Is this the kitten which you adopted last month?

A: Yes, ...

b) Q: Is this the teacher who speaks five languages?

A: No, ...

c) Q: Are you wearing the socks which grandma knitted for you?

A: Yes, ...

d) Q: Is this the house that your parents bought?

A: No, ...

e) Q: Do you go to the party that is on the beach?

A: Yes, ...

oder:
www.schuelerhilfe.de
/gute-noten
CODE 8415

bearbeitet am .... zu erreichende Punktzahl: **17** erreichte Punktzahl des Schülers ....

➡ Ab **14** erreichten Punkten kannst du zum nächsten Test übergehen.

Test 76 ▸ Modal auxiliaries: *can* und *could*

Schwierigkeits-grad

A1 | **Verbinde die passenden Satzteile.** | 6

a) Can you	**1.** understand you. It's too loud in here.
b) My sister can	**2.** play the guitar?
c) Could you	**3.** call me at 10:00 am this morning?
d) I'm sorry, but I can't	**4.** go to work today, because he was feeling sick.
e) Could you please	**5.** speak Spanish very well.
f) My brother couldn't	**6.** explain this to me again, please?

A2 | **Wähle die korrekte(n) Antwort(en) aus.** | 9

a) In welchen Fällen wird die Form *could* anstatt *can* verwendet?
   1) Wenn es um Möglichkeiten geht. ☐
   2) Wenn man sich in der Höflichkeitsform ausdrücken möchte. ☐
   3) Wenn man *can* in der Vergangenheit ausdrücken möchte. ☐
   4) Wenn man um Erlaubnis bitten möchte. ☐

b) Was ist die richtige Übersetzung für *she couldn't*?
   1) sie konnte etwas ☐
   2) sie war nicht in der Lage (etwas zu tun) ☐
   3) sie könnte nicht ☐
   4) es war ihr nicht erlaubt (etwas zu tun) ☐

c) Was ist die richtige Übersetzung für den folgenden Satz? „Mein Onkel kann sieben Sprachen sprechen."
   1) My uncle can speak seven languages. ☐
   2) My uncle could speak seven languages. ☐

d) Was ist die richtige Übersetzung? „Stopp, du kannst noch nicht reinkommen!"
   1) Stop, you couldn't come in yet. ☐
   2) Stop, you can't come in yet. ☐

e) In welchen Sätzen ist es möglich, den Satz mit dem Modalverb *could* zu bilden?
   1) My brother is allowed to drive the car today. ☐
   2) My brother was able to drive the car today. ☐
   3) My brother might drive the car today. ☐

oder:
www.schuelerhilfe.de/gute-noten
CODE 4669

---

bearbeitet am ▯▯▯   **zu erreichende Punktzahl: 15**   **erreichte Punktzahl des Schülers** ▯▯▯

➥ Ab **12** erreichten Punkten kannst du zum nächsten Test übergehen.

Schwierigkeits-
grad

A 1   Schreibe die folgenden Sätze um, indem du ein passendes modales Hilfsverb verwendest *(can, can't, could oder couldn't).*   5

a)   I am able to dance Salsa.

....

b)   My best friend Sarah got the opportunity to work abroad as an Au Pair.

....

c)   Am I allowed to go into the room?

....

d)   I was not able to see the moon in the sky.

....

e)   My aunt Annie doesn't know how to speak French.

....

A 2   Entscheide, ob die Form *could* oder *couldn't* am besten in die Lücke passt.   6

a)   We .... eat at the restaurant Mamma Mia. It is not too expensive.

b)   My mother .... change the appointment. They were very flexible.

c)   I .... use the mixer. I didn't find it anywhere.

d)   .... you buy some apples at the supermarket, please?

e)   I .... pick you up from school today, it is on my way back home.

f)   My best friend .... go to piano lesson today, because she broke her finger.

A 3   Entscheide, ob die Form *can* oder *can't* am besten in die Lücken passt.   3

a)   My 3-year-old cousin .... already ride a bike.

b)   I .... meet you tonight. I have an important appointment.

c)   We .... go by train, because it is too expensive.

oder:
www.schuelerhilfe.de
/gute-noten
CODE   4669

bearbeitet am   zu erreichende Punktzahl: 14   erreichte Punktzahl des Schülers

➡ Ab **11** erreichten Punkten kannst du zum nächsten Test übergehen.

© ZGS Bildungs-GmbH   *Englisch 7/8* ▪ 83

LE 6: Die modalen Hilfsverben – Modal Auxiliaries

Test 78 — Modal auxiliaries: *can* und *could*

A 1 Schreibe zu den Fragen eine passende Kurzantwort mit dem modalen Hilfsverb. | 4 |

a) Could you also buy tomatoes and bread at the supermarket? (+)

....

b) Can you walk backwards on a straight line? (+)

....

c) Can your brother drive a car? (–)

....

d) Could you send the photos to me per mail? (–)

....

A 2 Bringe die Wörter in die richtige Reihenfolge. Benutze auch die modalen Hilfsverben | 5 |
can, can't, could, couldn't.

a) reach · the · book · I · on · not · bookshelf · the

....

b) I · join · to · doctor · the · you

....

c) help · you · your · please · with · sister · cake · the · baking · ?

....

d) we · come · party · not · unfortunately · tcnight · the · to

....

e) do · not · my · I · homework · yesterday

....

oder:
www.schuelerhilfe.de
/gute-noten
CODE 4669

bearbeitet am | zu erreichende Punktzahl: 9 | erreichte Punktzahl des Schülers

➡ Ab **7** erreichten Punkten kannst du zum nächsten Test übergehen.

© ZGS Bildungs-GmbH | *Englisch 7/8* · 84

Test 79 — Modal auxiliaries: *may* und *might*

Schwierigkeits-
grad

A 1   Entscheide ob *may* oder *might* verwendet werden muss und umkreise die richtige Lösung.   8

a)   *May / might* I go to the shops and buy some sweets?

b)   You *may / might* go now and take my car if you like.

c)   I would love to go to the park at the weekend. But it *may / might* rain.

d)   I *may / might* not finish my homework by tonight. I will let you know.

e)   We *may / might* not be able to go to the zoo if Sam is still ill tomorrow.

f)   I left the door open and the dog ran out. Susi *may / might* not be pleased.

g)   I feel a bit unhealthy today. I *may / might* not go outside.

A 2   Kreuze den richtigen Satz an.   8

a)   ☐ You *may* have to read the text several times.
    ☐ You *might* have to read the text several times.

b)   ☐ I *might* have a big cake for my birthday.
    ☐ I *may* have a big cake for my birthday.

c)   ☐ Sam and I *may* go to Italy in our holidays.
    ☐ Sam and I *might* go to Italy in our holidays.

d)   ☐ If I had trusted him from the beginning, things *may* have been different.
    ☐ If I had trusted him from the beginning, things *might* have been different.

e)   ☐ *May* I help you with your bags?
    ☐ *Might* I help you with your bags?

f)   ☐ Next time you *might* try to be on time.
    ☐ Next time you *may* try to be on time.

A 3   Entscheide ob *may* oder *might* verwendet werden muss und umkreise die richtige Lösung. Für jede richtige Lösung gibt es einen Punkt.   6

Susi, a young pupil aged sixteen, wanted to go abroad for 6 months to an English-speaking county. Her father was quite proud about his daughter's courage, but her mother was worried if she would manage to travel alone. Her mother *may / might* have hoped for Susi to change her mind, but Susi had always wanted to do what was best for herself. She *may / might* have listened to her mother when she was younger. A few weeks later, Susi had made up her mind and announced that she was going to Australia. Her father seemed to be happy for her, but her mother *may / might* have been more delighted if her daughter would stay in Europe. The week after, all family members started with the preparations for Susi's travel. Her father said: We *may / might* have to get you a new Rucksack, the old one is too small. As a response, her mother added: You *may / might* also want to buy a new pair of shoes. After some months, Susi started her travel to Australia, with a quick stop in Singapore. She enjoyed her trip and *may / might* go to Australia again someday.

oder:
www.schuelerhilfe.de
/gute-noten
CODE   5194

bearbeitet am   zu erreichende Punktzahl: 24   erreichte Punktzahl des Schülers

➡ Ab **19** erreichten Punkten kannst du zum nächsten Test übergehen.

Test 80 Modal auxiliaries: *may* und *might*

Schwierigkeits-grad

A1 **Entscheide ob *may* oder *might* verwendet werden muss und umkreise die richtige Lösung.** 8

a) *May / might* I eat two pieces of cake?

b) You *may / might* have to be quiet, when you come home in the night.

c) Susi loves to go swimming, but she is feeling ill and *may / might* have to stay at home.

d) We *may / might* not feel like cooking today. I think we will order some food.

e) My family lives all over the world. I *may / might* have to spend my birthday alone.

f) I forgot to take the rubbish out. My mother *may / might* not be pleased.

g) Sam wasn't very nice to me yesterday. I *may / might* not go to his party.

A2 **Kreuze den richtigen Satz an.** 8

a) ☐ We *may* have to eat at home. The restaurant is too crowded.
☐ We *might* have to eat at home. The restaurant is too crowded.

b) ☐ Jane *might* have to write the test again.
☐ Jane *may* have to write the test again.

c) ☐ My sister and I *may* travel to Australia next year.
☐ My sister and I *might* travel to Australia next year.

d) ☐ If she had found out earlier, things *may* have been different.
☐ If I she had found out earlier, things *might* have been different.

e) ☐ If you *may* have been more careful, the food wouldn't have fallen down.
☐ If you *might* have been more careful, the food wouldn't have fallen down.

f) ☐ *May* I have more tea, please.
☐ *Might* I have more tea, please.

g) ☐ Next week you *may* try to finish your homework.
☐ Next week you *might* try to finish your homework.

A3 **Entscheide ob *may* oder *might* verwendet werden muss und umkreise die richtige Lösung. Für jede richtige Lösung gibt es einen Punkt.** 9

A lot of children want to have a pet at home. Some children *may / might* choose to have a little animal they can play with. Their parents *may / might* think about getting a Hamster or a Guinea pig. But this *may / might* not be the best choice. Some people say, you *may / might* not trust a cat. They *may / might* scratch you in the face. A dog *may / might* be a good option, but you must have enough time to take care of it. Finding a pet *may / might* not be as easy as you think. There are several things you must think about. You *may / might* want to think everything through before you buy a pet. Finding the suitable pet, *may / might* be a very important decision for your future.

oder:
www.schuelerhilfe.de
/gute-noten
CODE 5194

bearbeitet am **zu erreichende Punktzahl: 25** **erreichte Punktzahl des Schülers**

➡ Ab **20** erreichten Punkten kannst du zum nächsten Test übergehen.

Test 81   Modal auxiliaries: *may* und *might*

Schwierigkeits-
grad

A1 Entscheide ob *may* oder *might* verwendet werde muss und umkreise die richtige Lösung.   **8**

a)   The electrical parts of the coffee machine *may / might* not come into contact with liquids.

b)   This fantastic story*may / might* not come true.

c)   Credit cards *may / might* not be accepted by some shops.

d)   In case of emergency it *may / might* be necessary to stop the train.

e)   In winter it *may / might* become difficult to go to school by bike.

f)   If the weather is hot, the horses *may / might* not want to go into the stable.

g)   The children *may / might* not be familiar with the new computer.

A2 Kreuze den richtigen Satz an.   **4**

a)   ☐ The children *may* have to follow the adults.
     ☐ The children *might* have to follow the adults.

b)   ☐ It *might* become impossible to ride the bike as it snows heavily.
     ☐ It *may* become impossible to ride the bike as it snows heavily.

c)   ☐ If you are late you *may* miss the beginning of the play.
     ☐ If you are late you *might* miss the beginning of the play.

d)   ☐ If we go by car, we *may* arrive earlier than the others.
     ☐ If we go by car, we *might* arrive earlier than the others.

A3 Entscheide ob *may* oder *might* verwendet werde muss und umkreise die richtige Lösung.   **9**

During the summer holidays many families go to the sea. They *may / might* rent a flat near the beach. The children *may / might* go swimming or diving. Some *may / might* even attend surfing lessons. Many games can be played at the beach. Some children *may / might* play football, badminton or volley ball. The parents *may / might*t like to spend the day sunbathing.

A lot of people love travelling to Spain. This *may / might* be because of the sunny weather, friendly people and Mediterranean food. But Italy is also a frequently visited country. A lot of people *may / might* like to visit Rom or Venice. Some people *may / might*   want to visit the Colosseum. But others *may / might* want to have a boat trip.

bearbeitet am [   ]   zu erreichende Punktzahl: 21   erreichte Punktzahl des Schülers [   ]

➡ Ab **17** erreichten Punkten kannst du zum nächsten Test übergehen.

Test **82**   Modal auxiliaries: *must* oder *need*

Schwierigkeits-
grad

A 1 **Wähle die richtige/n Antwort/en aus und kreuze sie an.**   7

a) Wann wird nicht das modale Hilfsverb *must*, sondern das Verb *to have to* verwendet?

  1) In anderen Zeitformen. *Must* steht immer nur im *Simple Present*. ☐

  2) Mit der 3. Person Singular *(he, she, it)*. ☐

b) Welche der folgenden Sätze stehen in der richtigen Form?

  1) I do not need to study today. ☐

  2) I not need to study today. ☐

  3) I needn't study today. ☐

  4) I need not study today. ☐

  5) I studyn't today. ☐

  6) I don't need to study today. ☐

  7) I don't needn't study today. ☐

c) Welche Aussagen sind richtig?

  1) *mustn't* bedeutet: etwas nicht müssen ☐

  2) *mustn't* bedeutet: etwas nicht dürfen ☐

  3) Das Verb *to be allowed to* kann ein Ersatz für das Modalverb *mustn't* sein. ☐

A 2 **Fülle die Lücken mit den verneinten Modalverben *needn't* oder *mustn't*.**   7

a) We .... eat at the Italian restaurant. We can also eat burgers.

b) My sister .... go out tonight. Our parents are angry at her.

c) I .... do any homework today.

d) Children .... drink alcohol.

e) People .... cross the street at red traffic lights. It's dangerous.

f) Children .... watch a movie with age restrictions alone.

g) People .... take their pets into this hotel.

oder:
www.schuelerhilfe.de
/gute-noten
CODE   9094

bearbeitet am ⬚   zu erreichende Punktzahl: 14   erreichte Punktzahl des Schülers ⬚

➡ Ab **11** erreichten Punkten kannst du zum nächsten Test übergehen.

Test 83 — Modal auxiliaries: *must* oder *need*

Schwierigkeits-
grad

A1 **Fülle die Lücken mit den Modalverben *must, mustn't* und *needn't*.** 6

a) I .... buy new tooth paste. I don't have anything left.

b) Jonathan .... play football today. His team has an important match today.

c) Maria .... go to school today. It's Sunday.

d) You .... buy more apples. There are still 6 left.

e) You .... be late for school! The teacher will get angry.

f) Marc .... drive a car yet. He isn't 18 years old yet.

A2 **Bringe die Wörter in die richtige Reihenfolge. Verwende auch *must* oder *need*.** 4

a) sister · essay · finish · tonight · her · my

....

b) Dan · any · eat · not · milk products

....

c) supervisor · tomorrow · meet · I · my

....

d) I · not · today · homework · any · do

....

A3 **Ersetze die Verben mit den modalen Hilfsverben *must* und *need*.** 6

a) My sister is not allowed to go to this party tonight. Our parents are angry at her.

....

b) Children are not allowed to use the roller coaster alone.

....

c) Ben has to call his girlfriend as soon as he arrives.

....

d) Visitors are not allowed to bring their own food and drinks into the cinema.

....

e) Hotel guests are not allowed to celebrate parties in their hotel rooms.

....

f) Pupils do not have to do any homework during the weekend.

....

oder:
www.schuelerhilfe.de
/gute-noten
CODE 9094

bearbeitet am _____ zu erreichende Punktzahl: 16   erreichte Punktzahl des Schülers _____

➡ Ab **13** erreichten Punkten kannst du zum nächsten Test übergehen.

Test **84**   Modal auxiliaries: *must* oder *need*

Schwierigkeits-
grad

A1   **Schreibe die Sätze zu Fragen um. Benutze hierfür wenn möglich das modale Hilfsverb.** | 7

a) I must play tennis today.

....

b) I need to buy some beer before going to the party.

....

c) My sister must be at the train station on time.

....

d) She mustn't go to the cinema today.

....

e) We must eat at the restaurant Mamma Mia tonight.

....

f) We need to bring Ben to his friend's place.

....

g) Your brother must play the guitar now.

....

A2   **Bringe die Wörter in die richtige Reihenfolge. Verwende auch *must* oder *need*.** | 3

a) Jenny · vocabulary · practice · Spanish · today · a lot · the

....

b) we · visit · colleague · tonight · your · ?

....

c) the children · not · this room · Christmas · enter · before

....

oder:
www.schuelerhilfe.de
/gute-noten
CODE   9094

bearbeitet am   **zu erreichende Punktzahl: 10**   **erreichte Punktzahl des Schülers**

➡ Ab **8** erreichten Punkten kannst du zum nächsten Test übergehen.

© ZGS Bildungs-GmbH   *Englisch 7/8* · **90**

Test 85 Modal auxiliaries: *should*

Schwierigkeits-
grad

A1 Deine Mutter hat dir eine Liste mit Dingen geschrieben, die du erledigen sollst. | 5
Bilde für jeden Punkt einen Satz mit dem Modalverb *should*.

To-do-list:

– do your homework
– do not make a mess in the house
– talk to grandma
– play with your brother Ben
– do not watch too much T.V.

Love, mum

a) ....

b) ....

c) ....

d) ....

e) ....

A2 Was ist die alternative Form von *should*? Kreuze die richtige Version an. | 1

a) You have to tidy up your room.   ☐

b) You ought to tidy up your room.   ☐

c) You can tidy up your room.   ☐

A3 Kreuze an, ob es sich bei dem Satz um einen Ratschlag, eine Forderung/Verpflichtung oder | 5
eine Wahrscheinlichkeit handelt.

a) Where is Jane? – Don't worry, she should be here in a minute.
☐ Ratschlag
☐ Forderung/Verpflichtung
☐ Wahrscheinlichkeit

b) You should be more active and do sports to support your health.
☐ Ratschlag
☐ Forderung/Verpflichtung
☐ Wahrscheinlichkeit

c) He is such a bad person, he should be punished.
☐ Ratschlag
☐ Forderung/Verpflichtung
☐ Wahrscheinlichkeit

d) You should spend more time together so you have shared memories.
☐ Ratschlag
☐ Forderung/Verpflichtung
☐ Wahrscheinlichkeit

e) Why are you here? You should be at school right now!
☐ Ratschlag
☐ Forderung/Verpflichtung
☐ Wahrscheinlichkeit

oder:
www.schuelerhilfe.de
/gute-noten
CODE   2375

bearbeitet am | zu erreichende Punktzahl: 11   erreichte Punktzahl des Schülers |

➡ Ab **9** erreichten Punkten kannst du zum nächsten Test übergehen.

Test 86 **Modal auxiliaries: *should***

Schwierigkeits-
grad

A 1 **Verbinde die Satzteile, sodass sich sinnvolle Sätze ergeben.** `5`

a) Grandma should

b) We should

c) Little Martin should

d) You should

e) I should

clean our house before Christmas.

learn more for school.

stop working and start playing with my kids.

see the doctor soon.

spend more time with me.

A 2 **Schreibe die fehlenden Wörter in die Lücken.** `6`

Grandpa is telling us what his parents taught him about life. "They said, I .... always surround me

with people with whom I feel comfortable. People who make me feel bad .... be real friends. Then

they told me I .... spend too much time on finding the perfect job because there are more

important things than money. I .... be around 30 years old when I start planning kids because you

.... have lived your own life before giving birth to someone new. In the end they said

I .... simply stay as I am because that was how they loved me."

A 3 **Bilde mit Hilfe der Satzbausteine ganze Sätze und ergänze das Modalverb *should*.** `5`
**Entscheide dann, ob der jeweilige Satz eine Wahrscheinlichkeit, einen Ratschlag oder eine
Forderung/Verpflichtung ausdrückt.**

a) work less · spend more time · my parents · tney · with me · can · so

....

b) say sorry · you · go · to your friend · and

....

c) be · in June · on vacation · we

....

d) at your party · that loud · you · not · be

....

e) I · done · with school · be · 2025 · before · not

....

oder:
www.schuelerhilfe.de
/gute-noten
CODE `2375`

---

bearbeitet am .... zu erreichende Punktzahl: 16 erreichte Punktzahl des Schülers ....

➡ Ab **13** erreichten Punkten kannst du zum nächsten Test übergehen.

© ZGS Bildungs-GmbH *Englisch 7/8* ▪ 92

Test 87 Modal auxiliaries: *should*

Schwierigkeits-
grad

A1 Übersetze die Sätze ins Englische. | 5

a) „Mama, du solltest dich beruhigen."

....

b) Ich sollte gerade in der Schule sein, aber ich bevorzuge es im Bett zu bleiben.

....

c) Dieses Jahr Weihnachten sollte es keinen Schnee geben.

....

d) Mein Bruder soll Oma beim Kochen helfen, aber er will nicht.

....

e) „Ihr solltet euch den Fernseher kaufen, wenn er so gut in euer Wohnzimmer passt."

....

A2 Bilde aus den Satzbausteinen je zwei Sätze mit den Modalverben *should* und *ought to*. | 6

a) to the supermarket · I · now · go

....

b) Sam · go and look · isn't here · if · for him · in one hour · we

....

c) you · mum · not · wake up

....

A3 Wie könnte man diesen Satz umformulieren, sodass er einen Ratschlag, eine Forderung/Verpflichtung oder eine Wahrscheinlichkeit ausdrückt? | 3

„You read this book."

a) ....
b) ....
c) ....

oder:
www.schuelerhilfe.de
/gute-noten
CODE 2375

bearbeitet am .... zu erreichende Punktzahl: 14 erreichte Punktzahl des Schülers ....

➡ Ab **11** erreichten Punkten kannst du zum nächsten Test übergehen.

Test 88   Modal auxiliaries: *to be able to*

Schwierigkeits-
grad

A 1   **Verbinde die passenden Satzteile miteinander.**   5

a)   Grandma   am not able to help mum and dad in the kitchen yet.

b)   Together we   is not able to cook dinner for us.

c)   Dad   is able to pick us up from every training we want to join.

d)   I   are able to celebrate a great party for my birthday.

e)   Mum   is able to bake the best cake ever.

A 2   **Kreuze jeweils die richtige Form von *to be able to* an.**   4

a)   Next week I .... play soccer again.
     ☐ am able to
     ☐ was able to
     ☐ have been able to
     ☐ will be able to

b)   My parents .... encourage me whenever I am sad.
     ☐ are able to
     ☐ were able to
     ☐ have been able to
     ☐ will be able to

c)   My brother .... get on my nerves since he was born.
     ☐ is able to
     ☐ was able to
     ☐ has been able to
     ☐ will be able to

d)   When we were young, we .... stay up all night to play video games.
     ☐ are able to
     ☐ were able to
     ☐ have been able to
     ☐ will be able to

A 3   **Lies die Sätze und benenne die Zeitform, in der *to be able to* steht.**   4

a)   We have always been able to have lots of fun together.

     ....

b)   Last Sunday you were able to make an important goal for the team.

     ....

c)   In winter I will be able to go ice skating.

     ....

d)   "Dad, you are able to fix the T.V., aren't you?"

     ....

oder:
www.schuelerhilfe.de
/gute-noten
CODE   2974

bearbeitet am   **zu erreichende Punktzahl: 13**   **erreichte Punktzahl des Schülers**

➡ Ab **10** erreichten Punkten kannst du zum nächsten Test übergehen.

Test 89 — Modal auxiliaries: *to be able to*

Schwierigkeits-grad

A 1 Sarah soll sich für ihre Bewerbung Gedanken darüber machen, welche Fähigkeiten sie hat und welche nicht. Fülle die Lücken mit den richtigen Formen von *to be able to.* | 5

a) I am Sarah, a sixteen-year-old girl who .... do her job as expected from her.

b) When I have to learn I .... focus on my studies.

c) Sometimes mum .... (not) make me come to dinner because I want to finish my homework first.

d) My friends say that I .... find the right words to explain mathematics to them.

e) But I think I .... (not) become a teacher one day.

A 2 Setze die richtige Form von *to be able to* in die Lücken ein. | 5

a) You .... able to play guitar.

b) They .... able to go climbing since they were six years old.

c) Yesterday grandma .... able to show us how to bake her special cake.

d) Next year I .... able to start studying.

e) Last week mum .... able to go to the cinema with us.

A 3 Marc hat einen schlechten Tag und zweifelt daran, dass er das Schuljahr schaffen kann. Du möchtest ihm Mut machen und zählst dafür all seine Fähigkeiten auf, die du an ihm schätzt. Schreibe für jeden Stichpunkt einen Satz mit der richtigen Zeitform von *to be able to.* | 5

Marc's abilities

- always finds the right words when I am sad
- great football player since always
- motivated me when I was unsure about the test in mathematics last week
- gives right answers to the teacher even if he has no clue what he's talking about
- makes fun out of every situation since I've known him

a) ....

b) ....

c) ....

d) ....

e) ....

oder:
www.schuelerhilfe.de
/gute-noten
CODE 2974

bearbeitet am .... zu erreichende Punktzahl: 15 erreichte Punktzahl des Schülers ....

➡ Ab **12** erreichten Punkten kannst du zum nächsten Test übergehen.

Test **90** — Modal auxiliaries: *to be able to*

Schwierigkeits-
grad

A1 **Übersetze die Sätze, indem du die richtige Zeitform von *to be able to* verwendest.**   4

a) Ihr könnt sehr schön singen.

....

b) Ich erinnere mich, dass du schon immer gut malen konntest.

....

c) Als Oma und Opa jünger waren, konnten sie noch häufiger reisen.

....

d) Nächstes Wochenende wird super, weil wir dann zusammen übernachten können.

....

A2 **In dieser Aufgabe siehst du Bilder von Anna, die zeigen, was sie alles kann,**   12
beziehungsweise nicht kann. Bilde jedes Mal einen Satz mit *to be able to* im *Simple Present*,
***Simple Past*, *Present Perfect* und *will-future*.**

a) ....
....
....
....
....
....

b) ....
....
....
....
....

c) ....
....
....
....
....
....

oder:
www.schuelerhilfe.de
/gute-noten
CODE   2974

bearbeitet am _____   **zu erreichende Punktzahl: 16**   **erreichte Punktzahl des Schülers** _____

➡ Ab **13** erreichten Punkten kannst du zum nächsten Test übergehen.

Das Passiv – The Passive Voice

Test 91 · Das Passiv in verschiedenen Zeiten

Schwierigkeits-
grad

A1 Wähle die richtigen Antworten aus und kreuze sie an. 5

a) Wie wird das Passiv gebildet?
1) be + Infinitiv ☐
2) be + Past Participle ☐
3) to + Infinitiv ☐
4) to + Past Participle ☐

b) Welche Regeln gelten, wenn aus einem Aktivsatz ein Passivsatz gebildet werden soll?
1) Das Objekt aus dem Aktivsatz wird zum Subjekt im Passivsatz. ☐
2) Das Objekt aus dem Aktivsatz bleibt Objekt im Passivsatz. ☐
3) Das Subjekt im Aktivsatz bleibt das Subjekt im Passivsatz. ☐
4) Das Subjekt aus dem Aktivsatz wird zum Objekt im Passivsatz. ☐

c) Wann verwendet man die Passivform?
1) Wenn man sich höflich ausdrücken möchte. ☐
2) Wenn man nicht weiß, wer die Handlung durchführt. ☐
3) Wenn man das Objekt hervorheben möchte. ☐
4) Wenn man sich förmlich ausdrücken möchte. ☐

A2 Fülle die Lücken mit der richtigen Passiv-Form des Verbs. 8

a) The cake was _____ (to bake) by my sister.

b) The new lamp was _____ (to buy) by my dad.

c) The baby was _____ (to feed) by her mother.

d) The book was _____ (to write) by J.K. Rowling.

e) Yesterday, the door _____ (to lock) by Mr. Miller.

f) The store _____ (to open) by the shop assistant every day.

g) The computer _____ (to use / never) by Bob.

h) The speech _____ (to hold) by the Prime Minister in a few minutes.

oder:
www.schuelerhilfe.de
/gute-noten
CODE 4025

---

bearbeitet am _____ zu erreichende Punktzahl: 13 erreichte Punktzahl des Schülers _____

➡ Ab **10** erreichten Punkten kannst du zum nächsten Test übergehen.

Test 92 Das Passiv in verschiedenen Zeiten

Schwierigkeits-
grad

A1 Bestimme die Zeiten im Passivsatz. | 6

a) She has been fed this morning already.

....

b) The shop is opened at 9.00.

....

c) The new students will be welcomed by the teacher today.

....

d) This question was asked before.

....

e) The Italian restaurant of this city has been closed since last winter.

....

f) Today, he got fired.

....

A2 Beantworte die Fragen mit einem Passivsatz. | 7

a) Who will bring some vegetables? *(Lisa)*

....

b) Who has won the contest? *(His little brother)*

....

c) Who usually determines the new plans? *(committee members)*

....

d) Who wrote the poem? *(Polly)*

....

e) Did Jenny bake the cookies? *(Yes)*

....

f) Did your mum pick you up from school? *(No)*

....

g) Could you take a photo of me? *(Yes)*

....

oder:
www.schuelerhilfe.de
/gute-noten
CODE 4025

bearbeitet am zu erreichen de Punktzahl: **13** erreichte Punktzahl des Schülers

➡ Ab **10** erreichten Punkten kannst du zum nächsten Test übergehen.

Test 93 Das Passiv in verschiedenen Zeiten

Schwierigkeits-grad

A1 **Verwandle die Aktivsätze, wenn möglich, in Passivsätze.**　　　8

a) Betty is writing a letter to her boyfriend.

....

b) I'm not going to complete the project before the deadline. I don't have enough time.

....

c) Her husband will prepare a big dinner tonight.

....

d) My grandpa repaired my car last week.

....

e) Ben is looking out of the window for three hours now.

....

f) My little sister usually asks me for help.

....

g) Many tourists have visited the museum.

....

h) The band is playing a song about hopeless love.

....

A2 **Bringe die Wörter in die richtige Reihenfolge. Verwende das Verb in der richtigen Zeitform**　　　6
und im Passiv.

a) the train station · her mother · by · to · bring · just · she

....

b) this garden · clean · since 1999 · Mr. Jones · by

....

c) half a year · construction site · the · finish · in

....

d) the exam · three teachers · check · by · next week

....

e) sell · shops · by · the mobile phone · five

....

f) my colleague · the bananas · by · buy · always

....

oder:
www.schuelerhilfe.de
/gute-noten
CODE　4025

bearbeitet am 　　　　　**zu erreichende Punktzahl: 14**　　**erreichte Punktzahl des Schülers**

➡ **Ab 11** erreichten Punkten kannst du zum nächsten Test übergehen.

Test 94 — Das Passiv in verschiedenen Zeiten

Schwierigkeits-
grad

A 1 Von den folgenden Antwortmöglichkeiten steht jeweils nur ein einziger Satz richtig im Passiv. Kreuze den richtigen Passivsatz an. | 4 |

a) The men built a ship. ☐

The men are built a ship. ☐

The ship is built by men. ☐

b) My parents are annoyed by my behaviour. ☐

My behaviour annoys my parents. ☐

My parents annoy by my behaviour. ☐

c) The cowboy rides by a horse. ☐

The cowboy has a horse. ☐

The horse is ridden by a cowboy. ☐

d) In California, fire destroys huge forests. ☐

In California, forests destroy huge fires. ☐

In California, forests are destroyed by huge fires. ☐

A 2 Fülle die Lücken mit der richtigen Form des Passiv im Präsens. | 8 |

a) Kevin .... (attack) by Joe.

b) The girl .... always .... (ignore) by the old dog.

c) Computers .... (use) all over the world.

d) Today, wales .... still .... (hunt) by Japanese boats.

e) YouTubers .... often .... (watch) by children.

f) Thieves .... (search) by the police.

g) Football .... (love) by many children in Germany and England.

h) English .... (learn) by most children across Europe.

oder:
www.schuelerhilfe.de
/gute-noten
CODE 4025

bearbeitet am .... zu erreichende Punktzahl: 12 erreichte Punktzahl des Schülers ....

➡ Ab **10** erreichten Punkten kannst du zum nächsten Test übergehen.

Test 95 — Das Passiv in verschiedenen Zeiten

Schwierigkeits-
grad

A1   Kreuze die Sätze an, die in einer *Progressive*-Form des Passivs stehen. | 4

a) She has been hunted by zombies. ☐

b) You are being attacked by aliens. ☐

c) Patricia is running a marathon this summer. ☐

d) Cats are being loved by farmers. ☐

e) Sometimes rushing to the bus is a good idea. ☐

f) After offering a coffee, my friend decided to give me tea instead. ☐

g) Dancers are being admired by a lot of people. ☐

h) The Netherlands were having trouble with storms in the winter. ☐

i) Barack Obama may still be working for the USA. ☐

j) He was being cherished by many Americans when he was President. ☐

A2   Fülle die Lücken mit dem Passiv der Zeitformen, die in Klammern stehen. | 10

a) Cookies _____ (to bake · *Simple Present*) by Mary.

b) Cats _____ (to attack · *Simple Past*) by big birds.

c) The children _____ (to teach · *Present Perfect*) by Mrs. Brown.

d) The house _____ (to strike · *Simple Past*) by a lightning.

e) Babies _____ always _____ (to love · *Simple Present*) by mothers.

f) Africa _____ (to rule · *Simple Past*) by different countries.

g) Meat _____ (to eat · *will-future*) less in 10 years.

h) Eagles _____ (to see · *Simple Past*) flying over the mountain.

i) Samantha _____ never _____ (to beat · *Present Perfect*) at tennis.

j) Children _____ (to regard · *Simple Present*) as the future.

oder:
www.schuelerhilfe.de
/gute-noten
CODE 4025

bearbeitet am _____   zu erreichende Punktzahl: 14   erreichte Punktzahl des Schülers _____

➡ Ab **11** erreichten Punkten kannst du zum nächsten Test übergehen.

Test 96 — Das Passiv in verschiedenen Zeiten

Schwierigkeits-
grad ■ ■ ■

A 1 Bei einigen Sätzen ist die Zeit im Passiv falsch gebildet worden. Korrigiere in ganzen Sätzen und schreibe den Namen der richtigen Zeitform in die Lücke. `10`

a) Tomorrow, the boat had been repaired by the crew.

Correct sentence: ....

Tense: ....

b) Yesterday, many drivers are surprised by the snow on the motorway.

Correct sentence: ....

Tense: ....

c) After having run all day, the athletes were exhausted by the party.

Correct sentence: ....

Tense: ....

d) I remember last year when the tourists are caught in a hurricane.

Correct sentence: ....

Tense: ....

e) Australia will once be settled by English prisoners before more immigrants came.

Correct sentence: ....

Tense: ....

A 2 Übersetze ins Englische. Achte auf die richtige Zeit. `9`

a) Chris wurde beim Stehlen erwischt. ....

b) Autos wurden von den Deutschen erfunden. ....

c) Johns Frau wird beim Tennis von Monica geschlagen werden. ....

d) Jeremy wird regelmäßig ins Krankenhaus gebracht. ....

e) Die Blumen werden zuerst gegossen und dann geschnitten. ....

f) Jede Minute werden 50 neue Smartphones hergestellt. ....

g) Schottland wurde von den Wikingern erobert. ....

h) San Francisco wird von einem Erdbeben getroffen werden. ....

i) Die Erde wird seit langem durch Autos und CO_2 verschmutzt. ....

....

oder:
www.schuelerhilfe.de
/gute-noten
CODE 4025

---

bearbeitet am _____   **zu erreichende Punktzahl: 19**   **erreichte Punktzahl des Schülers** _____

➡ Ab **15** erreichten Punkten kannst du zum nächsten Test übergehen.

LE 7: Das Passiv – The Passive Voice

Test 97 Gebrauch modaler Hilfsverben

Schwierigkeits-grad

A1 Bringe die Wörter in die richtige Reihenfolge. `2`

a) must / The / cooked / be / soup

....

b) The / shouldn't / been / told / secret / have

....

A2 Bilde Passivsätze mit den Wörtern in Klammern. `6`

a) The bike must .... *(repair)*.

b) Her homework must .... *(finish)* at midnight.

c) Such a story shouldn't have .... *(tell)* to children.

d) Questions can .... *(ask)* by everybody.

e) Football can .... *(play)* by many boys.

f) People must .... *(warn)* that there are lions.

A3 Forme den Aktivsatz in einen Passivsatz um. `7`

a) Somebody must wash the clothes.

....

b) Many people can speak English.

....

c) She can play the piano.

....

d) Tom must learn maths.

....

e) The teacher must open the window.

....

f) We should call a doctor.

....

g) The cat can eat a fish.

....

oder:
www.schuelerhilfe.de
/gute-noten
CODE `0855`

bearbeitet am [   ] **zu erreichende Punktzahl: 15** **erreichte Punktzahl des Schülers** [   ]

➡ Ab **12** erreichten Punkten kannst du zum nächsten Test übergehen.

Test 98 — Gebrauch modaler Hilfsverben

Schwierigkeits-
grad

A 1 **Verwandle die Aktivsätze ins Passiv.** 7

a) She can ride a bike.

....

b) He must learn this exercise.

....

c) They can drive a car.

....

d) I shouldn't start a relationship.

....

e) We must cook the spaghetti.

....

f) She can read a book.

....

g) He must catch the thief.

....

A 2 **Schreibe die Verben von Aufgabe 1 mit dem zugehörigen Modalverb heraus und stelle Aktiv** 7
und Passiv gegenüber.

a) ....

b) ....

c) ....

d) ....

e) ....

f) ....

g) ....

A 3 **Was verändert sich bei dem Modalverb und was verändert sich bei dem Verb, wenn man es** 1
ins Passiv umwandelt? Kreuze die richtige Antwort an.

a) ☐ Das Modalverb bleibt unverändert und das Verb ebenfalls.

b) ☐ Vor das Modalverb wird das Wort „be" eingesetzt, das Verb bleibt gleich.

c) ☐ Nach dem Modalverb wird das Wort „be" eingesetzt, das Verb steht in der dritten
Form.

oder:
www.schuelerhilfe.de
/gute-noten
CODE 0855

bearbeitet am ☐ **zu erreichende Punktzahl: 15** **erreichte Punktzahl des Schülers** ☐

➡ Ab **12** erreichten Punkten kannst du zum nächsten Test übergehen.

Test **99**   Gebrauch modaler Hilfsverben

Schwierigkeits-
grad

A1   **Forme die Aktivsätze ins Passiv um.**   12

a)   She can play a violin. ....

b)   Can she play a violin? ....

c)   We must listen to our parents. ....

d)   He can ride a motorcycle. ....

e)   We must clean the living room. ....

f)   They must play football. ....

g)   You should have studied the books. ....

h)   She should write a letter. ....

i)   You can do it alone. ....

j)   You should answer the questions. ....

k)   They must give children enough time. ....

l)   You must finish the work. ....

A2   **Gebe an, welche Form die richtige ist.**   2

a)   The opportunity .... by you.

    1)   may not be availed

    2)   may not have been availed

    3)   not may have been availed

b)   Should the book .... read by him?

    1)   been

    2)   have

    3)   have been

oder:
www.schuelerhilfe.de
/gute-noten
CODE   0855

bearbeitet am [   ]   **zu erreichende Punktzahl: 14**   **erreichte Punktzahl des Schülers** [   ]

➡ Ab **11** erreichten Punkten kannst du zum nächsten Test übergehen.

Test 100 Gebrauch modaler Hilfsverben

Schwierigkeits-
grad

A1 Ergänze die korrekte Verwendung von *can* und *should*. Achte auch auf Verneinung. 16

a) Peter is back in town. I _____ meet him.

b) Carla is so hungry. She _____ eat something.

c) Mum, it is really important to know, if Peter _____ go or not?

d) _____ you bring me some eggs? I want to bake a cake.

e) You _____ join if you want.

f) Lara looks done. She _____ go home.

g) I _____ run. It is late.

h) We _____ make a barbeque. The sun is out today.

i) They _____ calm down otherwise they will call the police.

j) _____ I eat the last piece of cake or not? What do you think?

k) The train is arriving.Lara is still in the bathroom. Even with all the power in the world,
   she _____ get it.

l) It _____ be nice if there is a nice place to sleep.

m) What do you think, _____ I write a book? I _____ write.

n) Marie forgot her smartphone. You _____ bring it back.

o) We will go for a hiking trip. I hope, we _____ sleep somewhere.

A2 Kreuze die richtigen Aussagesätze zu den Regeln der Modalverben an. 6

		richtig	falsch
a)	„Can" wird im Deutschen als „können" verstanden.	☐	☐
b)	„Must" wird in allen Zeitformen gleich verwendend.	☐	☐
c)	„Should" wird im Deutschen als „müssen" verstanden.	☐	☐
d)	Die meisten Modalverben haben einen angehängten Infinitiv.	☐	☐
e)	Sowie im Deutsch gibt es auch im Englischen eine unterschied-liche Verwendung der Modalverben.	☐	☐
f)	Will man „nicht müssen" ausdrücken, verwendet man „need not" verwenden anstatt von mustn't.	☐	☐
g)	had been staying	☐	☐

oder:
www.schuelerhilfe.de
/gute-noten
CODE 0855

bearbeitet am _____   zu erreichende Punktzahl: 22   erreichte Punktzahl des Schülers

➡ Ab **17** erreichten Punkten kannst du zum nächsten Test übergehen.

© ZGS Bildungs-GmbH   Englisch 7/8 ▪ 106

Test 101   Gebrauch modaler Hilfsverben

Schwierigkeits-
grad

A1   Verwende die richtige Form von *must, can* und *should*. Bedenke die Regeln für *must.* | 16

a) I .... (–) touch the porcelain from my grandparents because it is expensive.

b) She .... get a lot of money if she works really hard.

c) You .... (–) go out today. It is stormy.

d) We .... do our homework before we .... go out.

e) .... I have your biro?

f) They .... clean the whole house because they had a party.

g) Alma is a nice girl. You .... meet her.

h) I .... fix this for you. I am a good mechanic.

i) You .... keep quite before he will select you.

j) He .... play the piano.

k) She is so addicted to music. She .... learn to play the piano.

l) We .... spend a little bit more for the holiday to get a nice hotel.

m) I love this music group and they are coming close to our town. I .... buy a ticket.

n) She .... (–) spend as much as the pocket cost. So she leaves it in the shop.

o) I .... buy a car. I saved up.

A2   Entscheide, welche Sätze richtig und welche falsch sind. | 7

	richtig	falsch
a) I should have done my homework yesterday.	☐	☐
b) She cannot touch things in the museum. It is not permitted.	☐	☐
c) I must do the DJ this night.	☐	☐
d) We can bring food to the party. Everybody does.	☐	☐
e) I should read my mails every day to be informed.	☐	☐
f) They mustn't smoke in the aircraft. It is not permitted.	☐	☐
g) He must write the presentation this semester.	☐	☐

oder:
www.schuelerhilfe.de
/gute-noten
CODE   0855

bearbeitet am   zu erreichende Punktzahl: 22   erreichte Punktzahl des Schülers

➡ Ab **17** erreichten Punkten kannst du zum nächsten Test übergehen.

Test 102 ▸ Gebrauch modaler Hilfsverben

Schwierigkeits-
grad

A1 Setze in die Lücken folgende Modalverben ein. Beachte die Verwendung von *must* und seiner Verneinung.

24

can · cannot · should · should not · must · must not

I was born in a small village. So I .... declare myself as a guy out of town. When I went to New York it was like a fantasy. I said to my mum: "Finally, you .... just go down the street to get some food or other things you need in daily life."

She is now working at an office, which is also very close to the house of us. She .... have lunch with us every day. Also I .... go for a walk and pass by her without a long distance.

My new school is different as my old one. Now we .... do homework every day and we .... do a little bit more to get a good vote. At my old school it was always like we .... to but we don't .... do homework.

My friends of the class are always very stressed because there is always this: "You .... do more." For me it is more a good way to have discipline and to get the opportunity, that now my educations makes me well prepared, so I .... survive the coming job business much more better.

My dad is a leader of a journalistic company, but he is always ill and keeps out from work.

So he .... do a little bit more of his potential. He confirms always: "My doctor says, I .... do that high amount of work. My heart is stressed out." I .... believe him, but I .... He used to be like this, also at the old office.

The city itself is quite nice:that big, so many people within. There is a tram station, where you .... stay nearer then five meters, otherwise you would have been pushed by the crowd on the railway. I .... imagine how many people are passing every day that place.

If you come to New York, you .... visit all the nice places here. There are a lot. But you .... be very in time if you want to have a chance to fetch a look on the attractions.

Close to every quarter of a district there are a lot of parks. You .... do a lot of things there, but not everything. You .... play football in front of the pick-nick places. You .... cometo one, it is really nice to have one there. You .... skate in the skater corners, but there are many bad guys, so you .... do that. You .... also ride the bicycle, but you .... that on the greensides.

oder:
www.schuelerhilfe.de
/gute-noten
CODE 0855

bearbeitet am .... zu erreichende Punktzahl: 24 erreichte Punktzahl des Schülers ....

➡ Ab **19** erreichten Punkten kannst du zum nächsten Test übergehen.

© ZGS Bildungs-GmbH

Englisch 7/8 • **108**

Verben und Adjektive

Test 103 — Verben mit Adverbien und Präpositionen

Schwierigkeits-grad

A1 Kreuze an, welche Präpositionen zusammen mit dem Verb verwendet werden können. Es sind fast immer mehrere Antworten möglich.

15

	up	out	down	on	off	along	through	away	over
a) look									
b) turn									
c) take									
d) go									
e) hang									
f) pick									
g) tidy									
h) fall									
i) break									
j) sit									
k) blow									
l) get									
m) carry									
n) set									
o) write									

oder:
www.schuelerhilfe.de
/gute-noten
CODE 8895

bearbeitet am _____ zu erreichende Punktzahl: 15 erreichte Punktzahl des Schülers _____

➡ Ab **12** erreichten Punkten kannst du zum nächsten Test übergehen.

LE 8: Verben und Adjektive

Test 104 — Verben mit Adverbien und Präpositionen

Schwierigkeits-grad

A1 Ergänze die Sätze mit den richtigen Präpositionen. | 10

through · off · up · down · get · at · on · up · after · for

a) Put .... your jacket. It's cold outside.

b) Slow ...., we don't have to hurry.

c) Could you please pick me .... ?

d) I'm looking .... a new t-shirt. Can you help me?

e) How do you get .... with your parents?

f) Sorry that I'm late, I was held ....

g) My teacher helped me get .... the exercise.

h) Look .... her, she's beautiful.

i) It's hot. Why doesn't he take .... his jacket?

j) I must look .... the baby.

A2 Vollende die Sätze, indem du die passenden Wörter einfügst. | 10

look forward to · broke up · keep in touch · passed away · throw off · carry on · get going · get away · stand up · going down

a) I .... with him because he cheated on me.

b) We have to .... when you're on holiday.

c) He .... after he was ill for a long time.

d) I .... meeting up with my grandma.

e) I know you're sad but you have to ....

f) Hurry up! We have to .... or the plane leaves without us.

g) I really need to .... for a while and relax a little.

h) Will you please .... and leave?

i) She enjoys .... the hill to the lake.

j) .... your jacket! It is so warm today!

oder:
www.schuelerhilfe.de
/gute-noten
CODE 8895

bearbeitet am .... zu erreichende Punktzahl: 20 erreichte Punktzahl des Schülers ....

➡ Ab 16 erreichten Punkten kannst du zum nächsten Test übergehen.

© ZGS Bildungs-GmbH Englisch 7/8 · 110

Test 105 — Verben mit Adverbien und Präpositionen

Schwierigkeits-
grad

A1 Entscheide dich für die richtige Präposition und kreuze diese an. | 5

		on	off	up	to	in	at	after	for
a)	She tried her new shoes ...... and they fit.	☐	☐	☐	☐	☐	☐	☐	☐
b)	The parents are looking ...... their baby.	☐	☐	☐	☐	☐	☐	☐	☐
c)	I'm calling you ...... your mum's house.	☐	☐	☐	☐	☐	☐	☐	☐
d)	Don't take ...... your jacket. It is cold.	☐	☐	☐	☐	☐	☐	☐	☐
e)	Be sure to get ...... the train driving to Boston.	☐	☐	☐	☐	☐	☐	☐	☐

A2 Vervollständige die Sätze mit den passenden Präpositionen. | 9

a) We have to blow .... 10 balloons for your birthday.

b) My boyfriend and I broke .... because we argued a lot.

c) I will call you .... in ten minutes.

d) When we arrive at the airport, we have to check ....

e) You must find .... where she lives.

f) When my cousin grows .... , she wants to be a doctor.

g) I really need to sort .... my clothes.

h) The plane takes .... in two hours.

i) Please turn .... the TV, I want to watch a movie.

oder:
www.schuelerhilfe.de
/gute-noten
CODE 8895

bearbeitet am .... zu erreichende Punktzahl: 14 erreichte Punktzahl des Schülers ....

➡ Ab **11** erreichten Punkten kannst du zum nächsten Test übergehen.

Test 106 — Verben mit zwei Objekten

Schwierigkeits-grad

A1 Kreuze die korrekte Antwort an. Manchmal sind auch mehrere Antworten korrekt. [4]

a) Was ist die richtige Reihenfolge der Satzteile?

    1) SVOO – subject, verb, object, object   ☐

    2) SOVO – subject, object, verb, object   ☐

    3) OVSO – object, verb, subject, object   ☐

    4) VSOO – verb, subject, object, object   ☐

    5) VOSO – verb, object, subject, object   ☐

b) Was sind die speziellen Begriffe, um die Objekte zu benennen?

    1) Sachobjekt und Personenobjekt   ☐

    2) Präsensobjekt und Präteritumobjekt   ☐

    3) direktes Objekt und indirektes Objekt   ☐

    4) Singularobjekt und Pluralobjekt   ☐

c) Wie entscheidet man, welches der beiden Objekte zuerst im Satz steht?

    1) Das Objekt mit der wichtigsten Information steht immer am Satzanfang.   ☐

    2) Das Objekt mit der wichtigsten Information steht immer am Satzende.   ☐

    3) Es macht keinen Unterschied, welches Objekt zuerst im Satz steht, denn beide Wörter sind wichtig.   ☐

A2 Fülle die Lücken mit den richtigen Objekten. [9]

a) Jenny has bought _____ (lots of Christmas presents; for her friends).

b) She has brought _____ (the presents; to their Christmas dinner).

c) She has bought _____ (Lisa; a new pullover).

d) She has bought _____ (a new book; for Ben).

e) She has bought _____ (Tim; a new game).

f) Hey Lisa, can you show _____ (me; your new pullover)?

g) Ben, could you read _____ (the new book; to me)?

h) Tim, can you play _____ (your new game; with me)?

i) Lisa, Ben, and Tim give _____ (Jenny; a lot of hugs).

oder:
www.schuelerhilfe.de
/gute-noten
CODE 1003

bearbeitet am   zu erreichende Punktzahl: 13   erreichte Punktzahl des Schülers

➡ Ab **10** erreichten Punkten kannst du zum nächsten Test übergehen.

Test 107 Verben mit zwei Objekten

Schwierigkeits-
grad

A1 Markiere die Verben, die mit zwei Objekten stehen können. | 18

a)	to bring	j)	to kiss	s)	to lend
b)	to wear	k)	to light up	t)	to play
c)	to cook	l)	to ask	u)	to tidy up
d)	to name	m)	to show	v)	to tell
e)	to make	n)	to explain	w)	to translate
f)	to offer	o)	to tell	x)	to give
g)	to read	p)	to speak	y)	to sing
h)	to eat	q)	to write	z)	to send
i)	to type	r)	to put		

A2 Beantworte die Fragen mit einem korrekten Satz, der zwei Objekte enthält. | 7
Achte auch auf die richtige Reihenfolge der Objekte.

a) Who did Jenny buy a new stuffed animal for? *(her little brother)*

....

b) Who did Sarah tell the secret? *(her best friend)*

....

c) Who promised to keep the secret of Ben? *(Sarah)*

....

d) Who did Hannah send a birthday card to? *(her grandma)*

....

e) Who typed a love message to Ben? *(Charlotte)*

....

f) Who sold Jenny the stuffed animal? *(the friendly shop assistant)*

....

g) Did the shop assistant offer a good price to Jenny? *(Yes)*

....

oder:
www.schuelerhilfe.de
/gute-noten
CODE 1003

bearbeitet am | **zu erreichende Punktzahl: 25** | **erreichte Punktzahl des Schülers**

➡ Ab **20** erreichten Punkten kannst du zum nächsten Test übergehen.

Test 108 Verben mit zwei Objekten

Schwierigkeits-
grad

A 1 Bringe die folgenden Wörter in die richtige Reihenfolge, sodass ein korrekter Satz mit
zwei Objekten entsteht. Achte auch auf die richtige Zeitform des Verbs.

5

a) write · Lisa · every year · to her grandma · a Christmas card

_____

b) offer · the shop assistant · to clients · good price · never · for footballs

_____

c) give · Ben · his girlfriend · for the first time · yesterday · a kiss

_____

d) read · every evening · the mother · to her children · a chapter of the book

_____

e) explain · the recipe · to her grandchildren · grandma Rose · yesterday

_____

A 2 Verändere die Sätze so, dass du das Personenobjekt zum Subjekt machst.
Das vorherige Subjekt wird dann zum Personenobjekt.

5

a) Dan told Sarah a secret.

....

b) My mum showed me how to cook Lasagna.

....

c) My cousin sent me a picture of her trip to Spain yesterday.

....

d) The friendly man sold us a Christmas tree this morning.

....

e) My sister asked me about the party.

....

oder:
www.schuelerhilfe.de
/gute-noten
CODE 1003

bearbeitet am _____ zu erreichende Punktzahl: 10 erreichte Punktzahl des Schülers _____

➡ Ab **8** erreichten Punkten kannst du zum nächsten Test übergehen.

Test 109 — Adjektive als Substantive

Schwierigkeits-
grad

A 1 **Kreuze die richtige Antwort an.** `3`

a) Warum werden Adjektive substantiviert?

1) Weil sonst das Substantiv im Satz fehlen würde und der Satz dann nicht vollständig wäre. ☐

2) Um ein doppeltes Substantiv wegzulassen. So hört sich der Satz besser an und man vermeidet Wiederholungen. ☐

3) Sobald ein Adjektiv neben einem Substantiv steht, wird es automatisch substantiviert. ☐

b) Welche Antwort ist richtig?

1) Ein substantiviertes Adjektiv wird immer klein geschrieben. ☐

2) Ein substantiviertes Adjektiv wird immer groß geschrieben. ☐

3) Das substantivierte Adjektiv wird nur dann groß geschrieben, wenn es sich auf bestimmte Personen bezieht. ☐

d) Welche Antwort ist richtig?

1) Wenn ein Adjektiv substantiviert wird, steht es für einzelne Dinge oder Personen. ☐

2) Wenn ein Adjektiv substantiviert wird, steht es immer für mehrere Personen oder Dinge. ☐

3) Ein substantiviertes Adjektiv kann sowohl für einzelne Dinge und Personen als auch für Gruppen stehen. ☐

A 2 **Ersetze die Substantive, wenn möglich, durch ein substantiviertes Adjektiv.** `5`

a) The blonde girl has longer hair than me.

....

b) Rich people smoke less than poor people.

....

c) The younger people do more sports than the older people.

....

d) My older brother is taller than my younger brother.

....

e) The big apples are more expensive than the big pears.

....

oder:
www.schuelerhilfe.de
/gute-noten
CODE `6583`

bearbeitet am _____ zu erreichende Punktzahl: 8 erreichte Punktzahl des Schülers _____

➡ Ab **6** erreichten Punkten kannst du zum nächsten Test übergehen.

Test 110 Adjektive als Substantive

Schwierigkeits-
grad

A 1 **Kreuze die richtigen Antworten an.** | 4

a) Welche Antwort ist richtig?

1) Adjektive können nur in der Grundform substantiviert werden. ☐

2) Adjektive können nur in der Grundform und in der ersten Steigerung substantiviert werden. ☐

3) Adjektive können in der Grundform und in der ersten und zweiten Steigerungsform substantiviert werden. ☐

4) Adjektive können nur im Positiv und Superlativ substantiviert werden. ☐

5) Adjektive können im Positiv, Komparativ und Superlativ substantiviert werden. ☐

b) Welche Antwort ist richtig?

1) Substantivierte Adjektive brauchen die Pluralendung -s, wenn sie für Gruppen von Personen oder Dingen stehen. ☐

2) Wenn substantivierte Adjektive für einzelne Personen oder Dinge stehen, braucht das Verb des Satzes die Endung -s, um dieses zu signalisieren. ☐

3) Substantivierte Adjektive stehen immer ohne Pluralendung. ☐

4) Da substantiverte Adjektive immer für Gruppen von Dingen oder Personen stehen, steht auch das Verb des Satzes immer in der Pluralform. ☐

A 2 **Ergänze die fehlenden Formen zur Steigerung der Adjektive.** | 3

a) young · .... · ....

b) .... · .... · the healthiest

c) .... · worse · ....

A 3 **Bilde mit den vorgegebenen Wörtern aus Aufgabe 2 einen Satz. Benutze die Adjektive in der substantivierten Form.** | 3

a) .... have less job experience than ....

b) .... live the longest.

c) .... are more effective for your body. *(context of sports exercises)*

oder:
www.schuelerhilfe.de
/gute-noten
CODE 6583

bearbeitet am [   ]   zu erreichende Punktzahl: 10   erreichte Punktzahl des Schülers [   ]

➡ Ab **8** erreichten Punkten kannst du zum nächsten Test übergehen.

Test 111 Adjektive als Substantive

Schwierigkeits-
grad

A1 Wandle die substantivierten Adjektive in die passende Steigerungsform um. 3

a) My sister always tries to see the good in people.

....

b) Healthier food is often more expensive.

....

c) The old people often can't live in the fifth floor, if the house doesn't have an elevator.

....

A2 Substantiviere die Adjektive, wenn möglich. 3

a) Young women suffer from eating disorders more often.

....

b) Educated people often earn more.

....

c) The new child in our class is very intelligent.

....

A3 Bringe die Wörter in die richtige Reihenfolge. Verwende substantivierte Adjektive. 3

a) young people · old people · help · should

....

b) tall people · small people · are · beautiful · more · ?

....

c) friendly people · more · often · successful · are

....

oder:
www.schuelerhilfe.de
/gute-noten
CODE 6583

bearbeitet am ....   **zu erreichende Punktzahl: 9**   **erreichte Punktzahl des Schülers** ....

➡ **Ab 7** erreichten Punkten kannst du zum nächsten Test übergehen.

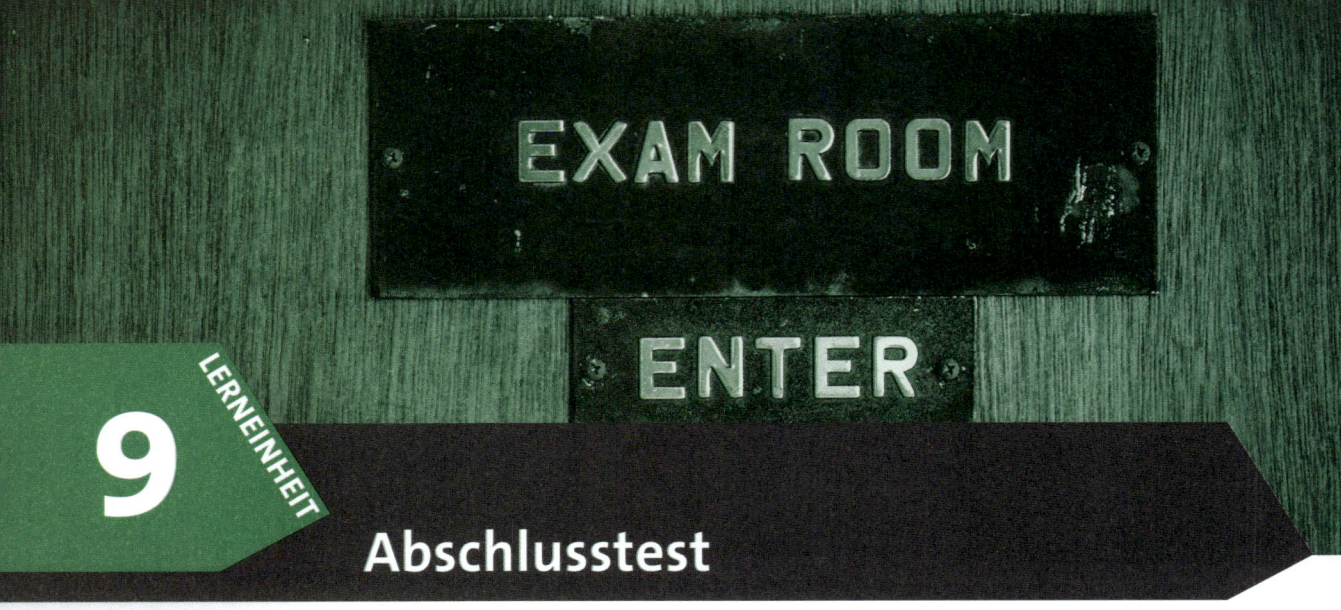

Test 112 ▸ Abschlusstest – Teil 1 von 3

Der Satzbau

A 1 **Wo ist der Satz richtig gebildet? Kreuze an.** | 4 |

a) ☐ I on Sundays my dog to play take out.
☐ On Sundays I take out my dog to play.
☐ My dog to play take out I on Sundays.

b) ☐ Does it rain every day in England?
☐ In England does every day it rain?
☐ Rain it does in England every day?

c) ☐ Don't they like to ride their old bikes.
☐ They don't like to ride their old bikes.
☐ Their like to don't ride they old bikes.

d) ☐ Not driving we are to the city right now.
☐ Are not we now to the city driving right.
☐ We are not driving to the city right now.

Die Zeitformen Simple Present und Present Progressive

A 2 **Vollende den Lückentext indem du die Verben in den Klammern entweder im** | 6 |
***Simple Present* oder im *Present Progressive* einträgst.**

a) The team _____ *(not play)* in the first football league, but it _____ *(win)* every match.

b) I _____ *(not watch)* TV because I _____ *(do)* my homework at the moment.

c) My teacher _____ *(like)* to read us stories and we always _____ *(want)* the story with the wizards.

d) Are we _____ *(listen)* to the radio and _____ *(play)* a game of cards right now?

e) They _____ *(read)* one book every week but Susan _____ *(read)* two books, because she is such a fast reader.

f) Their kids _____ *(not go)* to the party, because they _____ *(be)* mean right now.

Test 112   Abschlusstest – Teil 2 von 3

Die Zeitformen Simple Past und Past Progressive

A 3   Vollende den Lückentext indem du die Verben entweder im *Simple Past* oder *Past Progressive* einträgst.   `6`

a) While I _____ (play), the bus _____ (arrive).

b) Jonas _____ (become) sick while he _____ (travel).

c) _____ you _____ (go) to school yesterday?

d) _____ they _____ (wait) for her with the movie when

she _____ (come) too late?

e) She _____ (say) that she _____ (not feel) happy, so

I _____ (talk) to her.

f) What _____ you _____ (do) when

you _____ (hear) about 9/11?

Die Zeitform Present Perfect

A 4   Vollende den Lückentext indem du die Verben in den Klammern im *Present Perfect* einträgst.   `6`

a) The team mates _____ (not • forget) their games so far.

b) _____ she ever _____ (be) to Germany?

c) The mechanic _____ (repair) their car.

d) _____ Tim and Tom _____ (search) the house yet?

e) I _____ (buy) a new house today.

f) James _____ never _____ (go) to the butler school.

Die Zeitformen *going-to* Future und *will* Future

A 5   Vollende den Lückentext indem du die Verben in den Klammern entweder im going-to Future oder will Future einträgst.   `6`

a) They don't think they _____ (spend) their next vacation in Mexico.

b) The girls _____ (stay) at home tonight. Lisa and Trish are grounded.

c) It is strating to snow. I _____ (light up) the fire.

d) If you don't stop doing that I _____ (tell) mum!

e) It is late already. They _____ (miss) the show.

f) Look! He _____ (throw) the ball!

Die Verben

A 6 **Wo werden die richtigen Verbformen genutzt? Kreuze an.** ☐ 6

a) ☐ Can I go to the cinema, please?
☐ Must I go to the cinema, please?

b) ☐ She told them she might stay at home, but she wasn't sure.
☐ She told them she may stay at home, but wasn't sure.

c) ☐ He needn't take the car. It isn't that far.
☐ He mustn't take the car. It isn't that far.

d) ☐ She walk to school every day.
☐ She walks to school every day.

e) ☐ Open the window!
☐ Opens the window!

f) ☐ I can't swim. I've never learned it.
☐ I can swim. I've never learned it.

Der Gebrauch der verschiedenen Zeiten

A 7 **Umkreise die richtige Form des Verbs.** ☐ 4

a) I usually *go / am going / went / were going* to Judo on Mondays but not yesterday since *I have / am having / had / was having* a fever during practice time.

b) My mother *makes / is making / made / were making* the best pancakes and we *eat / are eating / ate / were eating* some while my father *work / is working / worked / was working*.

c) When I *come / am coming / came / was coming* from my vacation last week my little brother *is / is being / was / was being* ill.

d) Harry: "What *do / are doing / did / were doing* you want Sue?" Sue: "I *want / am wanting / wanted / were wanting* to know which route you usually *take / are taking / took / were taking* to school."

Die Pronomen

A 8 **Vollende den Lückentext indem du die richtigen Personal- oder Possessivpronomen einsetzt.** ☐ 6

a) Lisa: "Mr. Müller is .... teacher. .... is always late.

b) Max: " .... am Max this is .... brother Moritz. .... mother is

called Maria and .... are ten years old.

c) There are four dogs running to the river. .... try to cross it. Can you see .... ?

d) Joachim: "Hey Frank and Sabine! .... need .... help. Can ....

help .... ?"

e) Barbara: "Look at .... new game. .... can test .... !"

f) The Laumanns: "Do you know the Hartmann's dog? .... is big but .... , who

we have since 2005 is big, too.

Test 1 – Present Perfect – simple form

A1 7 Punkte

richtig: b), f)

A2 7 Punkte

a) Thomas has not missed the exam.

b) We have planted some trees in our garden.

c) We have sold our old car to friends of the family.

d) The train has left the station.

e) I have spent a lot of money.

f) He has read four sides of the newspaper.

g) You have driven much more slowly!

Test 2 – Present Perfect – simple Form

A1 10 Punkte

	positive	negative	question
a)	We have won.	We have not won.	Have we won?
b)	Paul has spent money.	Paul has not spent money.	Has Paul spent money?
c)	My wife has paid the bill.	My wife has not paid the bill.	Has my wife paid the bill?
d)	I have lost my keys.	I have not lost my keys.	Have I lost my keys?
e)	I have spoken.	I have not spoken.	Have I spoken?

A2 7 Punkte

a) Has the teacher corrected my mistakes?

b) Has my mother bought a new car?

c) Has the train left the station?

d) Has my neighbour sold his old car?

e) Have they cleaned up the kitchen?

f) Has the goalkeeper caught the ball?

g) Has the baby cried?

Test 3 – Present Perfect – simple Form

A1 15 Punkte

a) have eaten

b) have lost

c) went

d) haven't done

e) hasn't read

f) watched

g) have travelled

h) have seen

i) drove

j) haven't spent

k) haven't hidden

l) have taught

m) has danced

n) wrote

o) have learned

A2 7 Punkte

a) I went to Anna at nine o'clock yesterday.

b) Anna has baked a very delicious cake, now we eat it.

c) They have worked the whole day in the garden, now they are tired.

d) I drove to your house one hour ago.

e) Have you seen my passport in the kitchen?

f) I haven't seen it there.

g) I wasn't even in the house, I have just arrived.

Test 4 – Present Perfect Progressive

A1 11 Punkte

a) I have been playing video games all night.

b) She has been teaching English in a foreign country.

c) You have been calling me this morning.

d) We have been working one month four our presentation.

e) He has been composing three pieces of good classic music.

f) You have been weakening all of us.

g) We have been planning like fools.

h) They have been using wrong materials.

i) It has been producing a huge amount of products.

j) Theodor has been managing the crises and criminals of our jail.

k) I have been exercising all night.

A2 4 Punkte

a) You have not been watching a film.

b) Have I been losing my grammar skills?

c) Has she been waiting for a long time?

d) We have not been sailing on a very huge shipper.

Test 5 – Present Perfect Progressive

A1 14 Punkte

positive	negative	question
a) I have been asking something.	I have not been asking something.	Have I been asking something?
b) They have been meeting.	They have not been meeting.	Have they been meeting?
c) She has been cutting.	She has not been cutting.	Has she been cutting?
d) We have been tearing.	We have not been tearing.	Have we been tearing?
e) You have been noticing.	You have not been noticing.	Have you been noticing?
f) He has been repeating.	He has not been repeating.	Has he been repeating?
g) It has been diving.	It has not been diving.	Has it been diving?

A2   12 Punkte

a) I / (to listen to) / you
- ➥ I have been listening to you.
- ➥ I have not been listening to you.
- ➥ Have I been listening to you?

b) (to use) / a dictionary / he
- ➥ He has been using a dictionary.
- ➥ He has not been using a dictionary.
- ➥ Has he been using a dictionary?

c) around the garden / they / (to go)
- ➥ They have been going around the garden.
- ➥ They have not been going around the garden.
- ➥ Have they been going around the garden?

d) (to give up) / we
- ➥ We have been giving up.
- ➥ We have not been giving up.
- ➥ Have we been giving up?

e) you / in hospital / (to practice)
- ➥ You have been practicing in hospital.
- ➥ You have not been practicing in hospital.
- ➥ Have you been practicing in hospital?

f) with Clementine / Carla / (to differ)
- ➥ Carla has been disagreeing with Clementine.
- ➥ Carla has not been disagreeing with Clementine.
- ➥ Has Carla been disagreeing with Clementine?

Test 6 – Present Perfect Progressive

A1   22 Punkte

a) The journalist:
"Welcome, Charley. Excuse me. **Have you been waiting** for a long time?"

b) Charley Darn:
"Good morning. No, **I have only been waiting** for five minutes."

c) The journalist:
"Good. So, **have you immigrated** to Germany?"

d) Charley Darn:
"Yes, **I immigrated** five years ago."

e) The journalist:
"Oh really? And **have you been participating** in a project for cultures?"

f) Charley Darn:
"Yes, the project is called "Intercontinental Hugs". Up to now **it has had** such nice results."

g) The journalist:
"**You also wrote** a book, which **you have published** recently: A fantasy of "one world, no borders"?"

h) Charley Darn:
"**I have been** in a mood of very specific vision.

i) The journalist:
"And there **the idea came** up for your project?"

j) Charley Darn:
"Yes, **we thought of** something like a group around the world for cultural exchange."

k) The journalist:
"Very nice. So **we hope** that **your ideas anticipate** worldwide and **I saw** that you **have recorded** a soundtrack, which I am going to listen to right after this nice conversation."

l) Charley Darn:
"In fact, **we did.** Thank you. **It has been** a nice conversation."

m) The journalist:
"Thank you, too. **It was** an interesting interview!"

Test 7 – Present Perfect Simple und Present Perfect Progressive im Vergleich

A1   8 Punkte

a) has / have taken

b) has / have liked

c) has / have driven

d) has / have seen

e) has / have played

f) has / have spoken

g) has / have put

h) has / have met

A2 8 Punkte

a) has / have been writing

b) has / have been talking

c) has / have been showing

d) has / have been laughing

e) has / have been crying

f) has / have been watching

g) has / have been eating

h) has / have been drinking

A3 6 Punkte

a) My father **has never drunk** any alcohol.

b) The children **have been playing** videogames for three hours.

c) You are late. I **have been waiting** for a long time.

d) How long **have you known** your best friend?

e) He **has been studying** maths for hours.

f) **Has she worked / Has she been working** hard today?

Test 8 – Present Perfect Simple und Present Perfect Progressive im Vergleich

A1 2 Punkte

a) Ich möchte erzählen, was ich bis eben gemacht habe.
   ☒ I **have been talking** to her.
   ☐ I **have talked** to her.

b) Ich möchte mehr das Ergebnis der Handlung als den Verlauf betonen.
   ☒ She **has read** a book.
   ☐ She **has been reading** a book.

A2 4 Punkte

a) I (to talk):
   simple form ➡ I have talked.
   progressive form ➡ I have been talking.

b) He (to put):
   simple form ➡ He has put.
   progressive form ➡ He has been putting.

c) You (to eat):
   simple form ➡ You have eaten.
   progressive form ➡ You have been eating.

d) They (to drive):
   simple form ➡ They have driven.
   progressive form ➡ They have been driving.

A3 5 Punkte

a) My team has only lost two matches so far.

b) He has just finished his homework.

c) I have met three this week.

d) How long have you been waiting for me?

e) She has been playing this game since three o'clock.

Test 9 – Present Perfect Simple und Present Perfect Progressive im Vergleich

A1 16 Punkte

a) He (to drink) coke all day.
   1) He **has drunk coke** all day.
   2) He **has been drinking** coke all day.

b) I (not clean) the kitchen
   1) I **have not cleaned** the kitchen.
   2) I **have not been cleaning** the kitchen.

c) They (to discuss) all day.
   1) They **have discussed** all day.
   2) They **have been discussing** all day.

d) She (to think) about it.
   1) She **has thought** about it.
   2) She **has been thinking** about it.

e) We (to talk) about you.
   1) We **have talked** about you.
   2) We **have been talking** about you.

f) She (to live) in Germany, since she was seven years old.
   1) She **has lived** in Germany, since she was seven years old.
   2) She **has been living** in Germany, since she was seven years old.

A2 6 Punkte

a) She **has just arrived** at work.

b) He **has not been eating** fish all day.

c) I **have found** a new job.

d) He **has cut** his hair.

e) They **have been travelling** around Munich all day.

f) My grandpa **has stopped** drinking.

Test 10 – Past Perfect Simple

A1 15 Punkte

a) had read

b) had talked

c) had done

d) had spoken

e) had looked

f) had cooked

g) had argued

h) had discussed

i) had loved

j) had made

k) had drunk

l) had eaten

m) had bought

n) had driven

o) had listened

A2 4 Punkte

a) wrong ➡ had watched

b) right

c) right

d) wrong ➡ had argued

Test 11 – Past Perfect Simple

A1 6 Punkte

a) hadn't visited

b) had put

c) had ridden

d) hadn't travelled

e) had got/had gotten

f) hadn't found

A2 7 Punkte

a) had practised

b) had been

c) had not seen

d) had lived

e) had come

f) had made

g) had never seen

A3 5 Punkte

a) When I arrived at the cinema the film had started.

b) If you had listened to me, you would have passed the exam. / You would have passed the exam if you had listened to me.

c) She had met him somewhere before.

d) He had studied a lot for the exam.

e) She hadn't done her homework so she was in trouble.

Test 12 – Past Perfect Simple

A1 5 Punkte

a) he had eaten

b) she had danced

c) they had played

d) we had cooked

e) they had found

A2 5 Punkte

a) had bought

b) had liked

c) had been

d) had known

e) had died

A3 6 Punkte

a) He had laughed with his friend.

b) We had drunk with him.

c) She had sung with her.

d) You had said that to me / You had told me that.

e) He had played.

f) You had cooked.

Test 13 – Past Perfect Progressive

A1 11 Punkte

a) had been seeing

b) had been looking

c) had been driving

d) had been showing

e) had been knowing

f) had been drinking

g) had been eating

h) had been talking

i) had been watching

j) had been applying

k) had been washing

A2 6 Punkte

1) b   3) a   5) a

2) a   4) b   6) b

Test 14 – Past Perfect Progressive

A1 7 Punkte

a) right

b) wrong ➡ had been laughing

c) wrong ➡ had been watching

d) right

e) wrong ➡ had been shaking

f) wrong ➡ had been playing

g) right

A2 5 Punkte

a) She had been sleeping for 10 hours when you woke her up. / When you woke her up, she had been sleeping for 10 hours.

b) They had been watching TV for 30 minutes when you arrived. / When you arrived, they had been watching TV for 30 minutes.

c) How long had he been learning French before he went to Paris?

d) We had been waiting for the bus for 10 minutes when it started to rain. / When it started to rain, we had been waiting for the bus for 10 minutes.

e) He had been reading a comic when his mother came in. / When his mother came in, he had been reading a comic.

A3 6 Punkte

a) The cat had been eating a fish.

b) The dog had been drinking water.

c) They had been playing football.

d) We had been celebrating together.

e) You had been learning German.

f) She had been cleaning the kitchen.

Test 15 – Past Perfect Progressive

A1 8 Punkte

a) He had been washing his new car.

b) She had been riding her bike.

c) They had been eating a pizza.

d) I had been cooking spaghetti.

e) The dog had been looking out the window.

f) The cat had been playing with a mouse.

g) The baby had been sleeping.

h) Grandma had been reading a book.

A2 5 Punkte

a) had been visiting

b) had been speaking

c) had been answering

d) had been taking

e) had been eating

A3 3 Punkte

a) Had she been feeling good?

b) Had they been living in Cologne?

c) Had the policemen been catching the thief?

Test 16 – Verwendung von Past Perfect Simple und Past Perfect Progressive

A1 2 Punkte

a, d

A2 4 Punkte

a, b, d, e

A3 4 Punkte

a) She had won

b) We had swum

c) You had called

d) He had caught

Test 17 – Verwendung von Past Perfect Simple und Past Perfect Progressive

A1 4 Punkte

a, e, f, i

A2 7 Punkte

a) had been waiting

b) had been working

c) Had you been sleeping

d) had been carrying

e) had been phoning

f) had not been speaking

g) had been writing

Test 18 – Verwendung von Past Perfect Simple und Past Perfect Progressive

A1 5 Punkte

a) The storm destroyed the green fence that we had built.

b) My brother ate all the cookies I had made for him.

c) I had not been in the USA before 2015.

d) Had the bus left before you arrived?

e) Had you played with the dog in the garden before it started to rain?

A2 5 Punkte

a) Had you been sitting in the garden when I rang the bell?

b) I had not been living in London for five years.

c) We had been waiting for the waiter for 30 minutes.

d) The birds had been flying around when their human gave them their food.

e) I had been looking for my jeans all morning before I went to the supermarket.

Test 19 – Simple Present with future meaning

A1 4 Punkte

a) leaves   c) starts

b) arrive   d) opens

A2 8 Punkte

falsch: give, think

richtig: arrive, close, end, fly, open, leave

A3 1 Punkt

a) falsch

b) falsch

c) richtig

Test 20 – Simple Present with future meaning

A1 3 Punkte

a) does – leave

b) does not/doesn't arrive – arrives

c) do not/don't leave – leave

A2 6 Punkte

a) The bus leaves **tomorrow at 8 o'clock.**

b) Peter goes on a weekend trip with his football team **next weekend.**

c) The train arrives **at 6:30 in the morning.**

d) Jenny has a yoga class **on Wednesday in the morning.**

e) **Next Friday at 12 o'clock** there is an important Spanish exam.

f) The plane leaves **in 15 minutes.**

A3 6 Punkte

a) takes   d) begins

b) starts   e) Does … leave

c) does not leave / doesn't leave   f) has

Test 21 – Simple Present with future meaning

A1 5 Punkte

a) richtig   d) falsch

b) richtig   e) richtig

c) falsch

A2 6 Punkte

a) arrives   d) leaves

b) has   e) begins

c) does … open   f) arrives

Test 22 – Present Progressive with future meaning

A1 4 Punkte

a) richtig   c) richtig

b) falsch   d) falsch

A2 6 Punkte

a) is meeting   d) are eating

b) is flying   e) is going

c) are taking   f) am winning

A3 5 Punkte

a) We are going to the basketball match **tomorrow.**

b) **On Wednesday** I am leaving school earlier.

c) **Next week** Sarah is taking the train to visit her friend in Munich.

d) School is ending an hour later **on Friday** because of an event.

e) My friends are visiting me in hospital **on Saturday.**

Test 23 – Present Progressive with future meaning

8 Punkte

a) is not/isn't leaving

b) are – doing

c) am visiting

d) are – leaving

e) is – meeting

f) are taking

g) are not/aren't visiting

h) is making

A2 **4 Punkte**

a) On Thursday afternoon Charlotte is taking the train from Bochum to Bonn.

b) In the morning Bernd is helping his grandma with her household.

c) Alisa usually works on Mondays.

d) At noon they are having lunch later today.

Test 24 – Present Progressive with future meaning

A1 **7 Punkte**

1) On Saturday Jim is getting up ➡ d) at 7.00 am in the morning.

2) He is not having ➡ g) breakfast with his mother as usual because she is already working.

3) Jim's two sisters Sarah and Paula are meeting ➡ f) him at 9:00 am for breakfast in his kitchen.

4) His friend Josh is not coming ➡ b) to his house at 12.30 pm because he is late.

5) They are going ➡ c) to the basketball match all together by the bus.

6) At 7:30 pm they are playing ➡ e) against a very good team from Liverpool.

7) Later his co-player Adam is inviting ➡ a) all the other players to his house.

A2 **5 Punkte**

a) Tomorrow I am going to the city to buy new clothes.

b) I am going to visit my uncle in America next week.

c) Carol and Tim are taking the train to Berlin next week.

d) We are visiting a museum in Amsterdam on Monday with our class.

e) He is working on Saturday but it is no problem because I can do something on my own.

Test 25 – Das *going to-future*

A1 **6 Punkte**

a)	am	c)	is	e)	are
b)	are	d)	is	f)	are

A2 **4 Punkte**

a) Sarah isn't going to write the exam after lunch.

b) The neighbours aren't going to meet for a barbecue.

c) My brother isn't going to play soccer in the garden.

d) My classmates aren't going to study for maths together.

A3 **3 Punkte**

a) Yes, the Smiths are going to visit New York City this summer.

b) Yes, dad is going to listen to his favourite band tonight.

c) No, Julia and Stefan aren't going to go to the school ball tonight.

Test 26 – Das *going to-future*

A1 5 Punkte

a) (+) is going to be
(−) isn't/is not going to be

b) (+) are going to sleep
(−) aren't/are not going to sleep

c) (+) is going to say
(−) isn't/is not going to say

d) (+) are going to go
(−) aren't/are not going to go

e) (+) am going to hear
(−) am not going to hear

A2 4 Punkte

a) Is Clara going to become 15 years this Friday?

b) Are your parents going to buy a house at the beach?

c) Are the children going to win the match against the champion?

d) Is the cat going to jump onto the wall?

A3 4 Punkte

a) Yes, I am going to pass the exams at the end of the year.

b) Yes, the school is going to celebrate an anniversary this autumn.

c) No, she is not going to sing in the choir this semester.

d) No, it is not going to eat fruits for dinner.

Test 27 – Das *going to-future*

A1 4 Punkte

a) falsch   **b)** richtig   **c)** falsch   **d)** richtig

A2 5 Punkte

a) Are you going to do your homework tomorrow night?

b) When is dad going to wash the dishes?

c) How are the students going to solve the problem?

d) Is the doctor going to call the hospital?

e) Where are the children going to meet this weekend?

A3 9 Punkte

a) are you going to do

b) is going to go

c) are going to be

d) isn't/is not going to bark

e) is going to write

f) aren't/are not going to stay

g) is the plane going to start

h) is going to take

i) 'm / am going to ask

Test 28 – Das *will-future*

A1 2 Punkte

a) ☐ since, for

b) ☒ tomorrow, next month

c) ☐ always, every

d) ☐ last, yesterday

e) ☒ in 2022, the coming year

f) ☐ ever, before

A2 6 Punkte

a) Julia and I will talk to them tomorrow.

b) Will you help your father to tidy up the kitchen?

c) They will be back by 8:15 pm.

d) Will the festival take place this summer?

e) My parents will not punish/won't punish me for being late.

f) The Millers will not spend/won't spend Christmas in Sussex this year.

A3 5 Punkte

a) They'll read

b) He won't be

c) She'll never learn

d) We won't sing

e) I'll give

Test 29 – Das *will-future*

A1 5 Punkte

a) (+) will be   (–) won't be
b) (+) will sleep   (–) won't sleep
c) (+) will say   (–) won't say
d) (+) will go   (–) won't go
e) (+) will hear   (–) won't hear

A2 6 Punkte

a) richtig   d) falsch
b) falsch   e) richtig
c) richtig   f) richtig

A3 5 Punkte

a) richtig   c) falsch
b) richtig   d) richtig
e) falsch

Test 30 – Das *will-future*

A1 6 Punkte

a) richtig   d) falsch
b) falsch   e) richtig
c) richtig   f) richtig

A2 5 Punkte

a) Will it snow?
b) Will she forgive me?
c) What will they learn?
d) Won't the bus wait for us?
e) When will they leave?

A3 3 Punkte

a) falsch
b) richtig
c) richtig

Test 31 – Verwendung von Simple Present und Present Progressive

A1 9 Punkte

a) Simple Present   f) Present Progressive
b) Present Progressive   g) Simple Present
c) Simple Present   h) Present Progressive
d) Present Progressive   i) Simple Present
e) Simple Present

A2 3 Punkte

a) I am feeling good
b) He hurries up
c) They are lying

A3 4 Punkte

a) Usually, Ben doesn't finish his homework in time.
b) Right now, Daniel is washing the car.
c) Daniel wants to finish washing the car, but it takes a long time.
d) I am hiding the present under my bed.

Test 32 – Verwendung des Simple Present und Present Progressive

A1 12 Punkte

a) Simple Present   g) Present Progressive
b) Simple Present   h) Simple Present
c) Simple Present   i) Simple Present
d) Present Progressive   j) Present Progressive
e) Simple Present   k) Simple Present
f) Present Progressive   l) Simple Present

A2 3 Punkte

a) The bus leaves at 9:04am today.
b) Look! The brown cat is climbing up the tree.
c) Please wake up your brother.

A3 3 Punkte

a) Right now, I **am doing** my homework together with my cousin.

b) If you notice the light is chan**g**ing to green press that button.

c) My little brother watch**es** TV every morning.

Test 33 – Verwendung von Simple Present und Present Progressive

A1 6 Punkte

a) Right now I am not feeling well.

b) First I have maths, then I have biology, and after that I have arts lessons.

c) Everybody is looking outside, because it is snowing.

d) Yes, I am writing my essay right now.

e) No, dad isn't preparing the duck for Christmas dinner yet.

f) The bus to Berlin leaves at 13:00 today.

A2 5 Punkte

a) Mum is working in the garden while the toddlers are playing outside with the rabbits.

b) Tomorrow, Jim is cooking "Chicken Alfredo" for his family. He's already bought the ingredients.

c) The library closes during the night.

d) Thomas always goes to the bakery on Sundays.

e) While the rice is boiling you must chop the vegetables.

A3 5 Punkte

a) My piano lesson starts at 19:00 today.

b) Everybody is changing sides now because of the dangerous traffic.

c) The teacher is spelling the word so that everybody can write it down.

d) Nowadays, many children don't play outside so often anymore.

e) Children under the age of 16 are not allowed to watch this movie yet.

Test 34 – Verwendung von Present und Past Progressive

A1 7 Punkte

a) Present Progressive
b) Past Progressive
c) Past Progressive
d) Present Progressive
e) Present Progressive
f) Past Progressive
g) Present Progressive

A2 4 Punkte

a) you are checking
b) they were believing
c) he was dying
d) you are running

A3 4 Punkte

a) Right now, I am cooking dinner for my family.

b) Tomorrow, Sarah is washing her clothes. Everything is dirty!

c) During that workshop last week we were talking about body shaming.

d) Tom was tidying up his room, when his friend Ben entered.

Test 35 – Verwendung von Present und Past Progressive

A1 9 Punkte

a) Past Progressive
b) Present Progressive
c) Present Progressive
d) Present Progressive
e) Past Progressive
f) Present Progressive
g) Present Progressive
h) Past Progressive
i) Past Progressive

A2 4 Punkte

a) Yesterday, I was searching the internet for a present for my sister.

b) Right now, Ashley is preparing for her speech at work.

c) I was doing my homework some minutes ago.

d) He was flying on the plane while I was at school.

A3 **4 Punkte**

a) I am waiting in the mall now until the train arrives.

b) Yesterday, I was talking to my friend to ask about her opinion.

c) Are you already doing your homework?

d) How are you feeling right now?

Test 36 – Verwendung von Present und Past Progressive

A1 **5 Punkte**

a) Right now, I am watching a movie.

b) I was having a bad headache.

c) Today, we were doing some exercises.

d) While I was eating lunch, it started to snow.

e) I am drinking apple juice.

A2 **4 Punkte**

a) While I was answering the phone, the milk cooked over.

b) Right now, I am not feeling well.

c) He arrived home while Ben was doing the dishes.

d) Next week, I am going home by bus.

A3 **5 Punkte**

a) Yesterday, Debbie was tid**y**ing up her room.

b) Sarah is ru**nn**ing through the forest with her new shoes right now.

c) At the moment, I am wri**t**ing an essay about the 2nd world war.

d) Right now, Dan **is** kissing his girlfriend.

e) The singer at the concert last week **was** singing about his best friend.

Test 37 – Verwendung von Past und Past Perfect

A1 **9 Punkte**

a) Past Perfect

b) Simple Past

c) Simple Past

d) Past Perfect

e) Simple Past

f) Simple Past

g) Simple Past

h) Simple Past

i) Simple Past

A2 **8 Punkte**

a) to go – went – had gone

b) to put – put – had put

c) to buy – bought – had bought

d) to sell – sold – had sold

Test 38 – Verwendung von Past und Past Perfect

A1 **10 Punkte**

a) Past Perfect

b) Simple Past

c) Past Perfect

d) Simple Past

e) Past Perfect

f) Simple Past

g) Simple Past

h) Past Perfect

i) Past Perfect

j) Simple Past

A2 9 Punkte

a) Last year I **travelled** to Spain to visit my best friend.

b) My sister **started** baking the birthday cake after she **had done** the groceries.

c) Before that event last week, my best friend **had never lost** her passport.

d) Ben and David **finished** their homework two hours ago.

e) In 2012, our New Year's Eve **was** very boring.

f) After I **had been** in South America, I **went** to the USA.

g) My boyfriend **used to smoke** some years ago.

h) He **had never thought** about being in danger in his hometown before 9/11.

i) iLast week, Jenny **saw** a man breaking into her neighbor's house. Before that, she **had visited** her best friend Sarah, because she **had felt** sick. Afterwards, Jenny **told** Sarah everything.

Test 39 – Verwendung von Past und Past Perfect

A1 5 Punkte

a) we sat

b) they had built

c) you kept

d) I had studied

e) you had brought

A2 7 Punkte

a) Yesterday, it rained the whole day.

b) Two days ago, she had not started with the project yet.

c) I baked a cake for last week's tea time.

d) After he had done the groceries, he picked up his son from school.

e) Had you closed the windows before you left the house?

f) I had waited for you for two hours before I took the train home.

g) Last year, our Christmas dinner tasted very delicious.

A3 3 Punkte

a) Did you go to the bakery this morning after you had got up?

b) Yesterday, my best friend told me an interesting story.

c) Did you all understand that correctly?

Test 40 – Bedingungssätze – if-clauses Typ 1

A1 2 Punkte

a) ☐ b) ☒ c) ☒

A2 5 Punkte

a) If I **have** enough time, I will watch TV later this night.

b) Susan will visit her grandmother this afternoon, if she **catches** the train.

c) If the Smiths **are** late, they will miss the football game.

d) If Patrick **calls** this afternoon, I will ask him for dinner.

e) We will buy the new CD, if I **find** my purse.

A3 5 Punkte

a) If I give up smoking, I **will live** longer.

b) If they get married, everyone **will be** shocked.

c) If the students work harder, I am sure they **will get** marks.

d) If you get the job, they **will call** you right away.

e) If you see Professor Clever, you **must ask** him for his new book.

Test 41 – Bedingungssätze – if-clauses Typ 1

A1 5 Punkte

a) richtig

b) falsch

c) richtig

d) falsch

e) richtig

A2 **5 Punkte**

a) If the children **are** kind, they will get presents on Christmas Eve.

b) If Moritz **listens** carefully, he will get the answer.

c) If you **see** a witch in the forest, do not drink her magical drink!

d) He will talk about his latest idea, if you **visit** doctor Frankenstein.

e) An evil magician will lock you up, if you **look** into his eyes.

A3 **8 Punkte**

a) If I find her number, I **will call** her.

b) If Thomas does not go to school, he **will not meet** his friends.

c) If it snows, Julie and Sarah **will do** a ski course.

d) My husband **will not phone** my grandma, if I do not tell him to.

e) **Run** out of the house, if you hear the fire alert!

f) If somebody unknown knocks on the door, **do not open!**

g) If you fall into the pool, all people around **will laugh.**

h) If you go to bed early, you **can sleep** longer.

Test 42 – Bedingungssätze – if-clauses Typ 1

A1 **5 Punkte**

a) richtig

b) richtig

c) falsch

d) falsch

e) richtig

A2 **4 Punkte**

a) If you **use** SPLASH bubble bath, you **will feel** like a new-born baby.

b) If you **use** SOFT shampoo, you **will get** shiny hair.

c) If you **use** GENTLE soap, you **will get** softer skin.

d) If you **use** WIZARD vacuum cleaner, you **will spend** less time on housework.

A3 **6 Punkte**

a) If dad **buys** me an ice-cream, I **will wash** the dishes.

b) If my parents **win** a lot of money, we **will move** to a bigger house.

c) The students **can understand** Shakespeare, if the teacher **explains** the texts well.

d) If you **are able to come** to my party, you **will meet** some of my best friends.

e) I **will ask** for some advice, if I **have** problems.

f) If Kelly **finishes** her studies this year, she **will get** a good job in Tom's office.

Test 43 – Bedingungssätze – if-clauses Typ 1

A1 **7 Punkte**

a) I will go home

b) I will be very sad

c) I will be better in English

d) I will get more money

e) You will meet your friends

f) We will eat cake

g) You can meet your friends

A2 **9 Punkte**

a) If you play football

b) If the sun shines,

c) if I clean the kitchen

d) If Sandra doesn't feel good

e) if my mother earns enough money

f) if it rains.

g) If the weather is good

h) If she studies more

i) If I run a lot

A3 **10 Punkte**

a) are, will be

b) learn, will be

c) can leave, do

d) will help, need

e) leave, will follow

f) will visit, has

g) will cook, are

h) go, won't be

i) is, will go

j) meets, will eat

Test 44 – Bedingungssätze – if-clauses Typ 1

A1 **10 Punkte**

a) she will not get to know you.

b) we will not have a barbecue outside.

c) if I help my little sister.

d) If it snows

e) I will be tired the next day.

f) My legs will hurt

g) I will enjoy the sea

h) If we go to the restaurant

i) I will pick you up at 11 pm.

j) I will help you

A2 **10 Punkte**

a) do, will be

b) are, will visit

c) can ask, meet

d) will see, visits

e) miss, will take

f) is, will have

g) go, will spend

h) will leave, is

i) can take, are

j) will meet, takes

Test 45 – Bedingungssätze – if-clauses Typ 1

A1 **6 Punkte**

a) If you visit me, I will be very happy.

b) I will visit my friends, if my mother needs no help.

c) We will buy a new car, if we have enough money.

d) If my friend comes, we will eat cake.

e) If we get a cat, I will take care of it.

f) If we meet, we can have a dinner.

A2 **6 Punkte**

a) I will leave

b) If I have enough money

c) if I study more

d) I will go to Australia

e) I will be very relaxed.

f) if I need your help.

A3 **4 Punkte**

a) If she comes around, we will drink tea.

b) If she ignores me, I will be very sad.

c) If he is on time, we will get the train.

d) If you tidy up your room, you will visit your friends.

Test 46 – Bedingungssätze – if-clauses Typ 1

A1 **2 Punkte**

a) ☒

b) ☐

c) ☐

d) ☒

A2 5 Punkte

a) If I **had** time on Saturday, I would go to the cinema.

b) If the teachers **decided** to read the texts again, the pupils would have better chances.

c) She would participate in a party if they **realised** their party program.

d) Would you visit the zoo of London if you **were** there?

e) If grandpa **could** drive a car, he would buy himself a Ferrari.

A3 4 Punkte

a) The cats **would not eat** the birds on the tree if there was a dog in the garden.

b) If my family won one million euros, we **would not live** in a castle.

c) If Jenny's husband was a soldier, she **would not be** very happy.

d) Our school's athletes **would not win** the matches even if they practiced more.

Test 47 – Bedingungssätze – if-clauses Typ 1

A1 2 Punkte

a) ☒

b) ☐

c) ☒

d) ☐

A2 6 Punkte

a) If Lucy learned more for the test, she **would not / wouldn't get** a bad quote.

b) If I knew you were there, I **would bake** muffins.

c) **Would** you eat fish if you lived at the coast?

d) When **would** you **sleep** if you worked as a baker?

e) If you were a police officer, you **would** always **drive** carefully.

f) If dad sang the song, he **would not / wouldn't be** in the rhythm.

A3 4 Punkte

a) If Susanna **was** in the camp, she would become a sports teacher.

b) If the Millers **chose** the right door, they would win a car.

c) If Tom said the truth, Linda **would forgive** him.

d) If my French teacher taught us vocabulary, we **could speak** better.

Test 48 – Bedingungssätze – if-clauses Typ 2

A1 4 Punkte

a) If I was a movie star in Hollywood, I would be famous.

b) My hamster would not be fat, if I gave him good food.

c) My friends wondered what could happen, if someone kidnapped me in Brazil.

d) If he stopped playing this dangerous sport, he would still be healthy.

A2 4 Punkte

a) falsch ➡ He would get more attention, if he was not scared of girls.

b) richtig

c) falsch ➡ The boys would get good marks, if they did not talk all the time.

d) falsch ➡ If my sister got a cat, I would want to have a snake.

Test 49 – Bedingungssätze – if-clauses Typ 2

A1 7 Punkte

a) she would prepare dinner

b) I would travel around the world

c) I would meet her

d) she would visit us

e) I would see you

f) I would play football

g) I would visit you very often

A2 9 Punkte

a) If you were interested,

b) if I were rich.

c) If they liked tennis,

d) If you read more newspaper,

e) If you didn't lock your car,

f) if you listened to me.

g) if she did her homework.

h) If he exercised more,

i) If he left her,

A3 10 Punkte

a) were, would listen

b) had, would play

c) could buy, had

d) were, would order

e) were, could do

f) would go, were

g) would visit, didn't live

h) found, would bring

i) didn't invite, would be

j) didn't work, could not wok

Test 50 – Bedingungssätze – if-clauses Typ 2

A1 10 Punkte

a) If we had more time,

b) he would marry her.

c) if it rained.

d) I would save a lot of time.

e) if we were rich.

f) If my father knew this

g) I would go swimming with you.

h) We could meet each other

i) If I had a mobile phone

j) She would help you

A2 8 Punkte

a) did, would be

b) had, would buy

c) would do, lived

d) could buy, won

e) were, could get

f) went, would help

g) were, would go

h) met, would invite

Test 51 – Bedingungssätze – if-clauses Typ 2

A1 9 Punkte

a) if I had enough money

b) I would give

c) I would visit you

d) If I had a watch

e) I would meet her

f) I would leave

g) You would know her

h) if you were

i) He would be very happy

A2 8 Punkte

a) If I were taller, I would play basketball.

b) If you worked more, you would earn more money.

c) If I had a lot of money, I would buy a new bike.

d) If we talked more, we would know more about each other.

e) If I lost my bag, I would be very sad.

f) If I studied, I would pass the exam.

g) If I were you, I would call him.

h) If I knew his address, I would write him a letter.

Test 52 – Bedingungssätze – if-clauses Typ 3

A1 **2 Punkte**

a) ☐
b) ☐
c) ☐
d) ☒
e) ☒

A2 **4 Punkte**

a) If the children **had shouted** louder, the mother might have heard them.

b) We could have helped grandma if she **had told** us about her problems.

c) What would have happened if I **had become** president of the United States of America?

d) If the headmaster **had called** the parents yesterday, the pupils would not have gone to school this morning.

A3 **3 Punkte**

a) If I had not lost my purse, I **could have bought** new folders.

b) What **would have happened** if I had gone to university last year?

c) If Peter had decided to move earlier, he **might have lived** in a better flat.

Test 53 – Bedingungssätze – if-clauses Typ 3

A1 **1 Punkt**

a) ☐
b) ☒
c) ☐

A2 **4 Punkte**

a) If the German teacher had been less ill, we **would have read** the whole novel.

b) If Susan's husband had caught the ball, the window **would not have broken** into pieces.

c) James **would have sung** in the choir if the music teacher had asked him.

d) If my parents had not phoned Lisa, they **would not have known** about the party.

A3 **4 Punkte**

a) If I **had not lost** my bag, I **would not have called** the police.

b) The president **would not have given** a speech, if he **had not been** ill.

Test 54 – Bedingungssätze – if-clauses Typ 3

A1 **3 Punkte**

a) ☒   b) ☒   c) ☐   d) ☒

A2 **12 Punkte**

a) If I **had done** more work the night before, I **would have passed** it.

b) If I **had not gone to** the football game on Monday night, I **would not have felt** so tired on Tuesday.

c) If I **had phoned** him, he **would not have forgotten** to pick me up.

d) If I **had not jumped** down the stairs, my model **would not have fallen** down. If I **had had** the model in the lesson, the teacher **would have given** me a great mark.

e) If I **had told** her that I was coming home late, she **would not have been** mad and she **would not have waited** so long.

f) If I **had taken** the notice out, it **would not have been** wet.

A 3 3 Punkte

a) If the students had practised harder for the competition, they **would** have been faster.

b) If our school team had not been so slow, they **could** have caught the others.

c) If the weather conditions had not been so bad, they **might** have had a better chance.

Test 55 – Bedingungssätze – if-clauses Typ 3

A 1 7 Punkte

a) Typ 3

b) Typ 1

c) Typ 3

d) Typ 2

e) Typ 3

f) Typ 3

g) Typ 3

A 2 7 Punkte

a) If I had known you

b) if she had studied more

c) If you had visited her more often

d) If you had earned more money

e) if you had not been so angry

f) If he had exercised

g) if he had not eaten so much

A 3 6 Punkte

a) had left, would have got (gotten)

b) would have been, had met

c) had been, would have gone

d) had been, would have been

e) would have got (gotten), had been

f) would have had, had been

Test 56 – Bedingungssätze – if-clauses Typ 3

A 1 10 Punkte

a) I would not have eaten the pizza

b) if I had had more money

c) If I had had more time

d) She would have gone to work

e) if his mobile phone had not been broken

f) if your house had been cleaner

g) If she had learned more

h) he would not have left her

i) They would have been earlier

j) I would have bought you a present

A 2 10 Punkte

a) had visited, would have seen

b) would have opened, had had

c) would have baked, had known

d) had had, would not have taken

e) had talked, would have known

f) would have known, had bought

g) would have done, had not hurt

h) had not been, would have taken

i) would have had, had had

j) would have been, had not eaten

Test 57 – Bedingungssätze – if-clauses Typ 3

A 1 6 Punkte

a) had, have

b) taken

c) would, had

d) had

e) if

f) have

A2 6 Punkte

a) If we had learned more

b) we would have found a solution

c) I would have bought you a present

d) if he had lived next to me

e) If I had worked more

f) if you had asked me

A3 5 Punkte

a) If she had visited me, we would have been good friends.

b) If she had done her exercises, her mother wouldn't have been angry. / If she hadn't done her exercises, her mother would have been angry.

c) If we had got up earlier, we would have got the train.

d) If he had been friendly, he would have had more friends.

e) If he had saved money, he would have bought a car.

Test 58 – Relativsätze – relative clauses
mit *who, which* oder *that*

A1 3 Punkte

a) ☒

b) ☐

c) ☒

d) ☐

e) ☒

f) ☐

A2 4 Punkte

a) falsch

b) richtig

c) richtig

d) richtig

A3 7 Punkte

a) who

b) which

c) which

d) who

e) who

f) who

g) which

Test 59 – Relativsätze – relative clauses
mit *who, which* oder *that*

A1 8 Punkte

a) who, that

b) which, that

c) which, that

d) which, that

A2 5 Punkte

a) falsch

b) falsch

c) richtig

d) richtig

e) richtig

A3 6 Punkte

a) which/that

b) which/that

c) who/that

d) who/that

e) who/that

f) which

Test 60 – Relativsätze – relative clauses
mit *who, which* oder *that*

A1 7 Punkte

a) which

b) who

c) which

d) who

e) which

f) who

g) which

A2 4 Punkte

a) richtig

b) falsch

c) falsch

d) richtig

A3 4 Punkte

a) which/that often grow in the Caribbean

b) which/that was given to the USA by France

c) who/that works in a school

d) which/that people sleep in / in which people sleep

Test 61 – Relativsätze – relative clauses mit *who, which* oder *that*

A 1 7 Punkte

a)	☐	e)	☒	i)	☐
b)	☒	f)	☒	j)	☒
c)	☒	g)	☒		
d)	☐	h)	☒		

A 2 5 Punkte

a)	☒	d)	☒	g)	☒
b)	☐	e)	☒		
c)	☒	f)	☐		

Test 62 – Relativsätze – relative clauses mit *who, which* oder *that*

A 1 13 Punkte

a)	which	f)	who	k)	which
b)	who	g)	which	l)	who
c)	which	h)	who	m)	who
d)	which	i)	who		
e)	who	j)	who		

A 2 5 Punkte

a)	richtig	c)	richtig	e)	richtig
b)	falsch	d)	falsch		

Test 63 – Relativsätze – relative clauses mit *who, which* oder *that*

A 1 5 Punkte

a) A fir is a tree which is used as a christmas tree in December.

b) This parakeet is a male which has a blue nose.

c) Maja is a woman who likes to read.

d) This is my new computer which I bought last Saturday.

e) Donald Trump is America's president who is criticized all over the world.

A 2 6 Punkte

a) I have to paint my house which has red window frames.

b) I like the jeans which I bought yesterday.

c) He is the man who stole my heart nine years ago.

d) I lost my voice which is very strong.

e) Is this the man who wants to marry you?

f) Vegans are people who do not eat animal products.

Test 64 – Relativsätze – relative clauses mit *who, whose, who's* oder *whom*

A 1 7 Punkte

a)	who	d)	who	g)	Whose
b)	whose	e)	whose		
c)	who	f)	who		

A 2 6 Punkte

a) I know a girl. Her favourite sport is tennis.

b) This is the woman. She had an accident.

c) This is the first time we see that man. He's smoking a cigarette.

d) Do you like that boy? His favourite animals are dogs.

e) This is the boy. His car is very fast.

f) She is the one. I got the books from her.

Test 65 – Relativsätze – relative clauses mit *who, whose, who's* oder *whom*

A 1 5 Punkte

a) This is the girl who helped me with my homework.

b) This is the boy who studied maths with me.

c) This is my neighbour whose mother died.

d) This is a big city whose name is Munich.

e) This is my friend to whom I gave my laptop.

A2 6 Punkte

a) This is the man who baked the cake for us.

b) England is a country whose inhabitants speak English.

c) A policeman is a person who catches thieves.

d) A pilot is someone who's able to fly planes.

e) You have a baby who's crying the whole day.

f) A doctor is a person who can help other people.

A3 5 Punkte

a) who's

b) whose

c) who's

d) who's

e) who

Test 66 – Relativsätze – relative clauses mit *who, whose, who's* oder *whom*

A1 7 Punkte

a) Who

b) whose

c) who

d) who's

e) whom

f) who's

g) who

A2 6 Punkte

a) I sent an e-mail to my dad who lives in America.

b) I have a friend who feeds his cat with cheese.

c) The girl who's living next to me is always late.

d) Do you know that guy who's waiting at the bus stop?

e) We have a grandmother whose parents come from Russia.

f) Didn't I tell you the name of the person to whom I sent the email? / Didn't I tell you the name of the person who I sent the email to?

Test 67 – Relativsätze – relative clauses mit *who, whose, who's* oder *whom*

A1 12 Punkte

a) whose
b) who
c) who
d) whose
e) who
f) who
g) whose
h) whose
i) who
j) who
k) whose
l) who

A2 6 Punkte

a) richtig
b) falsch
c) richtig
d) richtig
e) richtig
f) falsch

Test 68 – Relativsätze – relative clauses mit *who, whose, who's* oder *whom*

A1 8 Punkte

a) who's
b) Who
c) whose
d) who
e) who
f) whose
g) who's
h) whose

A2 6 Punkte

a) Who's the best football player in the world?

b) Elliot is the man who broke my heart.

c) Magdalena is the woman whose children like to swim.

d) For whom did you bake the cookies?

e) To whom did the Millers go?

f) To whom this may concern

Test 69 – Relativsätze – relative clauses mit *who, whose, who's* oder *whom*

A1 7 Punkte

a) My sister who is pregnant is happy.

b) This is my friend Naomi who will bring us to the airport.

c) This is my aunt who's singing all day.

d) This is the old lady whose name is Sophia.

e) The old man, to whom I sold my house, died.

f) May I introduce you to my little sister who was born in 2010?

g) This is Kai who's the love of my life.

A2 5 Punkte

a) richtig   d) richtig

b) falsch   e) richtig

c) falsch

Test 70 – Relativsätze ohne Relativpronomen – contact clauses

A1 10 Punkte

a) Sandra is the girl who is standing next to Tim.

b) This is the boy I met yesterday.
    This is the boy who I met yesterday.

c) Have you seen my car which was parked next to the tree?

d) That's the girl who lives in Germany.

e) We met someone who was very tall.

f) The man you see in the red car is my dad.
    The man who you see in the red car is my dad.

g) The summer is the time of the year when it is warm outside.
    The summer is the time of the year it is warm outside.

A2 6 Punkte

a) This was an interesting book which I read the last week.

b) Do you like Anna who I met in High School?

c) This is my new mobile phone which I bought yesterday.

d) That's the boy who I remember well.

e) Do you see the girl who he's talking to?

f) This is the book which I got as a present.

Test 71 – Relativsätze ohne Relativpronomen – contact clauses

A1 7 Punkte

a) Sam is the boy I met yesterday.

b) This is my dog my parents gave to me on my last birthday.

c) This is my new car I bought last week.

d) I remember the article you told me about.

e) These are my parents I picked up at the airport.

f) The woman you see across the street is my mother.

g) Have you seen the people we met last weekend?

A2 8 Punkte

a) The dog **which** is playing with the ball is mine.

b) Tom is the boy **who** plays football.

c) Listen to the woman **who is** wearing the red pullover.

d) ☒

e) ☒

f) Anna is the girl **who** plays guitar.

g) ☒

h) This is the boy **who** lost his keys.

Test 72 – Relativsätze ohne Relativpronomen – contact clauses

A1 10 Punkte

a) –   f) –

b) who   g) who/that

c) where   h) –

d) which/that   i) which/that

e) whose   j) –

A2 9 Punkte

a) Anna is the girl we met yesterday.

b) That's my dog which is outside in the garden.

c) These are the boys I saw yesterday.

d) Here are your keys you lost 2 days ago.

e) This is the girl whose father works in a hospital.

f) Look at this cute rabbit I got as a present.

g) Listen to the woman who is wearing a red pullover.

h) That was my sister who was at the café yesterday.

i) This is the girl who travels to England.

Test 73 – Relativsätze ohne Relativpronomen – contact clauses

A1 5 Punkte

a) ☒   g) ☒

b) ☐   h) ☒

c) ☐   i) ☒

d) ☐   j) ☒

e) ☐   k) ☐

f) ☐

A2 5 Punkte

a) This is the window I cleaned yesterday.

b) This is the bike I bought in June.

c) Do you like the dress your mum bought for you?

d) This is the necklace I wanted for my birthday.

e) You are the man I've been looking for.

Test 74 – Relativsätze ohne Relativpronomen – contact clauses

A1 6 Punkte

a) The book I read has 1000 pages.

b) My favourite song, I listened to last night, was a hit in 1995.

c) The cat I love so much is sleeping in my bed.

d) The thriller I'm watching at the moment is very exciting.

e) Did you see the beautiful golden ring Anna wore last night?

f) Do you like the new jacket I bought for my son?

A2 6 Punkte

a) The boy who/that is looking at you is Paul.

b)

c)

d)

e) The baby who/that is crying is my cousin.

f)

Test 75 – Relativsätze ohne Relativpronomen – contact clauses

A1 12 Punkte

a)   e)   i) whose

b) whose   f) which   j)

c) who's   g) who   k)

d) which   h) which   l) whose

A2 5 Punkte

a) Yes, this is the kitten I adopted last month.

b) No, this isn't (is not) the teacher who speaks five languages.

c) Yes, I'm (I am) wearing the socks grandma knitted for me.

d) No, this isn't (is not) the house my parents bought.

e) Yes, I go to the party that is on the beach.

Test 76 – Modal auxiliaries: *can* und *could*

A1 6 Punkte

a) Can you play the guitar?

b) My sister can speak Spanish very well.

c) Could you explain this to me again, please?

d) I'm sorry, but I can't understand you. It's too loud in here.

e) Could you please call me at 10:00 am this morning?

f) My brother couldn't go to work today, because he was feeling sick.

A2 9 Punkte

a) **1)** Wenn es um Möglichkeiten geht.
   2) Wenn man sich in der Höflichkeitsform ausdrücken möchte.
   3) Wenn man *can* in der Vergangenheit ausdrücken möchte.

b) **2)** sie war nicht in der Lage (etwas zu tun)
   4) es war ihr nicht erlaubt (etwas zu tun)

c) **1)** My uncle can speak seven languages.

d) **2)** *Stop, you can't come in yet.*

e) **2)** My brother was able to drive the car today.
   3) My brother might drive the car today.

Test 77 – Modal auxiliaries: *can* und *could*

A1 5 Punkte

a) I can dance Salsa.

b) My best friend Sarah could work abroad as an Au Pair.

c) Can I go into the room?

d) I couldn't see the moon in the sky.

e) My aunt Annie can't speak French.

A2 6 Punkte

a) We **could** eat at the restaurant Mamma Mia. It is not too expensive.

b) My mother **could** change the appointment. They were very flexible.

c) I **couldn't** use the mixer. I didn't find it anywhere.

d) **Could** you buy some apples at the supermarket, please?

e) I **could** pick you up from school today, it is on my way back home.

f) My best friend **couldn't** go to piano lesson today, because she broke her finger.

A3 3 Punkte

a) My 3-year-old cousin **can** already ride a bike.

b) I **can't** meet you tonight. I have an important appointment.

c) We **can't** go by train, because it is too expensive.

Test 78 – Modal auxiliaries: *can* und *could*

als „Test war HA (wird „benote [handwritten]

A1 4 Punkte

a) Could you also buy tomatoes and bread at the supermarket? Yes, I could.

b) Can you walk backwards on a straight line? Yes, I can.

c) Can your brother drive a car? No, he can't.

d) Could you send the photos to me per mail? No, I couldn't.

A2 5 Punkte

a) I can't reach the book on the bookshelf. / I couldn't reach the book on the bookshelf.

b) I could join you to the doctor. / I can join you to the doctor.

c) Could you please help your sister with baking the cake?

d) Unfortunately, we can't come to the party tonight.

e) Yesterday, I couldn't do my homework.

Test 79 – Modal auxiliaries: *may* und *might*

A1 8 Punkte

a) may   d) might   g) might
b) may   e) might
c) might   f) might

A2 8 Punkte

a) may   c) might   e) might
b) may   d) might   f) might

A3 6 Punkte

may, might, might, may, might, might

Test 80 – Modal auxiliaries: *may* und *might*

A1 8 Punkte

a) may   d) might   g) might
b) might   e) may
c) might   f) might

A2 8 Punkte

a) may   d) may   g) might
b) might   e) might
c) might   f) may

A3 9 Punkte

may, might, might, may, may, might, might, may, may

Test 81 – Modal auxiliaries: *may* und *might*

A1 8 Punkte

a) may   d) may   g) might
b) may   e) may
c) might   f) might

A2 4 Punkte

a) might
b) may
c) might
d) may

A3 9 Punkte

may, may, might, may, may, may, might, may, may

Test 82 – Modal auxiliaries: *must* und *need*

A1 7 Punkte

a) 1) ☒
   2) ☐

b) 1) ☒
   2) ☐
   3) ☒
   4) ☒
   5) ☐
   6) ☒
   7) ☐

c) 1) ☐
   2) ☒
   3) ☒

A2 7 Punkte

a) We **needn't** eat at the Italian restaurant. We can also eat burgers.

b) My sister **mustn't** go out tonight. Our parents are angry at her.

c) I **needn't** do any homework today.

d) Children **mustn't** drink alcohol.

e) People **mustn't** cross the street at red traffic lights. It's dangerous.

f) Children **mustn't** watch a movie with age restrictions alone.

g) People **mustn't** take their pets into this hotel.

Test 83 – Modal auxiliaries: *must* und *need*

A1   6 Punkte

a) I **must** buy new tooth paste. I don't have anything left.

b) Jonathan **must** play football today. His team has an important match today.

c) Maria **needn't** go to school today. It's Sunday.

d) You **needn't** buy more apples. There are still 6 left.

e) You **mustn't** be late for school! The teacher will get angry.

f) Marc **mustn't** drive a car yet. He isn't 18 years old yet.

A2   4 Punkte

a) My sister must/needs to finish her essay tonight.

b) Dan mustn't eat any milk products.

c) I must/need to meet my supervisor tomorrow.

d) I needn't/don't need to do any homework today.

A3   6 Punkte

a) My sister **mustn't** go to this party tonight. Our parents are angry at her.

b) Children **mustn't** use the roller coaster alone.

c) Ben **must/needs to** call his girlfriend as soon as he arrives.

d) Visitors **mustn't** bring their own food and drinks into the cinema.

e) Hotel guests **mustn't** celebrate parties in their hotel rooms.

f) Pupils **needn't/don't need to** do any homework during the weekend.

Test 84 – Modal auxiliaries: *must* und *need*

A1   7 Punkte

a) Must I play tennis today?

b) Do I need to buy some beer before going to the party?

c) Must my sister be at the train station on time?

d) Is(n't) she allowed to go to the cinema today?

e) Must we eat at the restaurant Mamma Mia tonight?

f) Do we need to bring Ben to his friend's place?

g) Must your brother play the guitar now?

A2   3 Punkte

a) Jenny must/needs to practice the Spanish vocabulary a lot today.

b) Must we/Do we need to visit your colleague tonight?

c) The children mustn't enter this room before Christmas.

Test 85 – Modal auxiliaries: *should*

A1   5 Punkte

a) I/You should do my homework.

b) I/You should not/shouldn't make a mess in the house.

c) I/You should talk to grandma.

d) I/You should play with my/your brother Ben.

e) I/You should not/shouldn't watch too much TV.

A2   1 Punkte

b) You ought to tidy up your room.

A3   5 Punkte

a) Wahrscheinlichkeit

b) Ratschlag

c) Forderung/Verpflichtung

d) Ratschlag

e) Forderung/Verplfichtung

Lösungen

Test 86 – Modal auxiliaries: *should*

A1 5 Punkte

a) Grandma should see the doctor soon.

b) We should clean our house before Christmas.

c) Little Martin should learn more for school.

d) You should spend more time with me.

e) I should stop working and start playing with my kids.

A2 6 Punkte

should, shouldn't, shouldn't, should, should, should

A3 5 Punkte

a) My parents should work less so they can spend more time with me.
➡ Forderung/Verpflichtung

b) You should go and say sorry to your friend. / You should go to your friend and say sorry.
➡ Ratschlag

c) In June we should be on vacation. / We should be on vacation in June.
➡ Wahrscheinlichkeit

d) You shouldn't be that loud at your party.
➡ Ratschlag

e) I shouldn't be done with school before 2025.
➡ Wahrscheinlichkeit

Test 87 – Modal auxiliaries: *should*

A1 5 Punkte

a) "Mum, you should calm down."

b) I should be in school right now but I prefer staying in bed.

c) This Christmas there shouldn't be snow.

d) My brother should help grandma with cooking but he doesn't want to.

e) "You should buy this T.V. if it fits so well in your living room."

A2 6 Punkte

a) I should go to the supermarket now.
I ought to go to the supermarket now.

b) If Sam isn't here in one hour, we should go and look for him.
If Sam isn't here in one hour, we ought to go and look for him.

c) You should not/shouldn't wake mum up.
You ought not to wake mum up.

A3 3 Punkte

a) Ratschlag: "You should read this book, it's one of my favourites."

b) Forderung/Verpflichtung: "If you want to watch T.V. later you should read this book now."

c) Wahrscheinlichkeit: "In two weeks you should be done reading this book."

Test 88 – Modal auxiliaries: *to be able to*

A1 5 Punkte

a) Grandma is able to bake the best cake ever.

b) Together we are able to celebrate a great party for my birthday.

c) Dad is not able to cook dinner for us.

d) I am not able to help mum and dad in the kitchen yet.

e) Mum is able to pick us up from every training we want to join.

A2 4 Punkte

a) will be able to

b) are able to

c) has been able to

d) were able to

A3 4 Punkte

a) Present Perfect

b) Simple Past

c) will future

d) Simple Present

Test 89 – Modal auxiliaries: *to be able to*

A1 5 Punkte

a) is able to

b) am able to

c) is not able to

d) am able to

e) will not be able to

A2 5 Punkte

a) are

b) have been

c) was

d) will be

e) was

A3 5 Punkte

a) Marc is always able to find the right words when I am sad.

b) Marc has always been able to play football very well.

c) Last week Marc was able to motivate me when I was unsure about the test in mathematics.

d) Marc is able to give the right answers to the teacher even if he has no clue what he is talking about.

e) Since I've known him, Marc has been able to make fun out of every situation.

Test 90 – Modal auxiliaries: *to be able to*

A1 4 Punkte

a) You are able to sing very nice.

b) I remember that you have always been good at drawing.

c) When grandma and grandpa were younger, they were able to travel more often.

d) Next weekend is going to be great because we will be able to spend the night together.

A2 12 Punkte

a) **Simple Present:** Anna is able to ride her bike.
Simple Past: Anna was able to ride her bike.
Present Perfect: Anna has been able to ride her bike.
will-future: Anna will be able to ride her bike.

b) **Simple Present:** Anna is not able to dance ballet.
Simple Past: Anna was not able to dance ballet.
Present Perfect: Anna has not been able to dance ballet.
will-future: Anna will not be able to dance ballet.

c) **Simple Present:** Anna is able to bake cookies.
Simple Past: Anna was able to bake cookies.
Present Perfect: Anna has been able to bake cookies.
will-future: Anna will be able to bake cookies.

Test 91 – Das Passiv in verschiedenen Zeiten

A1 5 Punkte

a) 2)

b) 1); 4)

c) 2); 3)

A2 8 Punkte

a) The cake was baked by my sister.

b) The new lamp was bought by my dad.

c) The baby was fed by her mother.

d) The book was written by J.K. Rowling.

e) Yesterday, the door was locked by Mr. Miller.

f) The store is opened by the shop assistant every day.

g) The computer is never used by Bob.

h) The speech will be held by the Prime Minister in a few minutes.

Test 92 – Das Passiv in verschiedenen Zeiten

A1 6 Punkte

a) Present Perfect

b) Simple Present

c) will-future

d) Simple Past

e) Present Perfect

f) Simple Past

A2 7 Punkte

a) Some vegetables will be brought by Lisa.

b) The contest has been won by his little brother.

c) The new plans are usually determined by committee members.

d) The poem was written by Polly.

e) Yes, the cookies were baked by Jenny.

f) No, I wasn't picked up from school by my mum.

g) Yes, the photo could be taken by me.

Test 93 – Das Passiv in verschiedenen Zeiten

A1 8 Punkte

a) A letter is being written to her boyfriend by Betty.

b) The project isn't going to be completed before the deadline.

c) A big dinner will be prepared by her husband tonight.

d) My car was repaired by my grandpa last week.

e) –

f) Usually, I am asked for help by my little sister.

g) The museum has been visited by many tourists.

h) A song about hopeless love is being played by the band.

A2 6 Punkte

a) She has just been brought to the train station by her mother.

b) This garden has been cleaned by Mr. Jones since 1999.

c) The construction site will be finished in half a year.

d) The exam next week is going to be checked by three teachers.

e) The mobile phone is sold by five shops.

f) The bananas are always bought by my colleague.

Test 94 – Das Passiv in verschiedenen Zeiten

A1 4 Punkte

a) The ship is built by men.

b) My parents are annoyed by my behaviour.

c) The horse is ridden by a cowboy.

d) In California, forests are destroyed by huge fires.

A2 8 Punkte

a) Kevin is attacked by Joe.

b) The girl is always ignored by the old dog.

c) Computers are used all over the world.

d) Today, wales are still hunted by Japanese boats.

e) YouTubers are often watched by children.

f) Thieves are searched by the police.

g) Football is loved by many children in Germany and England.

h) English is learned by most children across Europe.

Test 95 – Das Passiv in verschiedenen Zeiten

A1   4 Punkte

a)	☐	f)	☐
b)	☒	g)	☒
c)	☐	h)	☐
d)	☒	i)	☐
e)	☐	j)	☒

A2   10 Punkte

a) Cookies are baked by Mary.

b) Cats were attacked by big birds.

c) The children have been taught by Mrs. Brown.

d) The house was struck by a lightning.

e) Babies are always loved by mothers.

f) Africa was ruled by different countries.

g) Meat will be eaten less in 10 years.

h) Eagles were seen flying over the mountain.

i) Samantha has never been beaten at tennis.

j) Children are regarded as the future.

Test 96 – Das Passiv in verschiedenen Zeiten

A1   10 Punkte

a) Correct sentence: Tomorrow, the boat will be repaired by the crew.
Tense: Will-future

b) Correct sentence: Yesterday, many drivers were surprised by the snow on the motorway.
Tense: Simple Past

c) Correct sentence: The sentence is already correct.
Tense: Simple Past

d) Correct sentence: I remember last year when the tourists were caught in a hurricane.
Tense: Simple Past

e) Correct sentence: Australia had once been settled by English prisoners before more immigrants came.
Tense: Past perfect

A2   9 Punkte

a) Chris was caught stealing.

b) Cars were invented by the Germans.

c) John's wife will be beaten at tennis by Monica.

d) Jeremy is constantly taken to hospital.

e) The flowers are first watered and then cut.

f) Every minute 50 new smartphones are being produced.

g) Scotland was invaded by the Vikings.

h) San Francisco will be hit by an earthquake.

i) The earth has been polluted by cars and CO_2 for a long time.

Test 97 – Gebrauch modaler Hilfsverben

A1   2 Punkte

a) The soup must be cooked.

b) The secret shouldn't have been told.

A2   6 Punkte

a) be repaired

b) be finished

c) have been told

d) be asked

e) be played

f) be warned

A3   7 Punkte

a) The clothes must be washed by somebody.

b) English can be spoken by many people.

c) The piano can be played by her.

d) Maths must be learned by Tom.

e) The window must be opened by the teacher.

f) A doctor should be called by us.

g) A fish can be eaten by the cat.

Test 98 – Gebrauch modaler Hilfsverben

A1 7 Punkte

a) A bike can be ridden by her.

b) This exercise must be learned by him.

c) A car can be driven by them.

d) A relationship shouldn't be started by me.

e) The spaghetti must be cooked by us.

f) A book can be read by her.

g) The thief must be caught by him.

A2 7 Punkte

a) can ride – can be ridden

b) must learn – must be learned

c) can drive – can be driven

d) shouldn't start – shouldn't been started

e) must cook – must be cooked

f) can read – can be read

g) must catch – must be caught

A3 1 Punkte

a) ☐

b) ☐

c) ☒

Test 99 – Gebrauch modaler Hilfsverben

A1 12 Punkte

a) A violin can be played by her.

b) Can a violin be played by her?

c) Parents must be listened to by us.

d) A motorcycle can be ridden by him.

e) The living room must be cleaned by us.

f) Football must be played by them.

g) The books should have been studied by you.

h) A letter should be written by her.

i) It can be done alone.

j) The questions should be answered by you.

k) Children must be given enough time.

l) The work must be finished.

A2 2 Punkte

a) 2)

b) 3)

Test 100 – Gebrauch modaler Hilfsverben

A1 16 Punkte

a) should

b) should

c) can

d) Can

e) can

f) should

g) should

h) can

i) should

j) Can

k) can't

l) can

m) should, can

n) should

o) can

A2 6 Punkte

		richtig	falsch
a)	„Can" wird im Deutschen als „können" verstanden.	☒	
b)	„Must" wird in allen Zeitformen gleich verwendend.	☒	
c)	„Should" wird im Deutschen als „müssen" verstanden.		☒
d)	Die meisten Modalverben haben einen angehängten Infinitiv.	☒	
e)	Sowie im Deutsch gibt es auch im Englischen eine unterschiedliche Verwendung der Modalverben.	☒	
f)	Will man „nicht müssen" ausdrücken, verwendet man „need not" verwenden anstatt von mustn't.	☒	

Test 101 – Gebrauch modaler Hilfsverben

A1 8 Punkte

a)	must not	f)	must	k)	should
b)	can	g)	should	l)	should
c)	should not	h)	can	m)	must
d)	must, can	i)	should	n)	must not
e)	Can	j)	can	o)	can

A2 7 Punkte

		richtig	falsch
a)	I should have done my homework yesterday.	☒	
b)	She cannot touch things in the museum. It is not permitted.		☒
c)	I must do the DJ this night.	☒	
d)	We can bring food to the party. Everybody does.		☒
e)	I should read my mails every day to be informed.	☒	
f)	They mustn't smoke in the aircraft. It is not permitted.	☒	
g)	He must write the presentation this semester.	☒	

Test 102 – Gebrauch modaler Hilfsverben

A1 24 Punkte

I was born in a small village. So I **can** declare myself as a guy out of town. When I went to New York it was like a fantasy. I said to my mum: "Finally, you **must** just go down the street to get some food or other things you need in daily life."

She is now working at an office, which is also very close to the house of us. She **can** have lunch with us every day. Also I **can** go for a walk and pass by her without a long distance.

My new school is different as my old one. Now we **must** do homework every day and we **should** do a little bit more to get a good vote. At my old school it was always like we **should** do but we don't have to do homework.

My friends of the class are always very stressed because there is always this: "You **should do** more." For me it is more a good way to have discipline and to get the opportunity, that now my educations makes me well prepared, so I **can** survive the coming job business much more better.

My dad is a leader of a journalistic company, but he is always ill and keeps out from work. So he **should** do a little bit more of his potential. He confirms always: "My doctor says, I **must** not do that high amount of work. My heart is stressed out." I **should** believe him, but I **can't**. He used to be like this, also at the old office.

The city itself is quite nice: that big, so many people within. There is a tram station, where you **must not** stay nearer then five meters, otherwise you would have been pushed by the crowd on the railway. I **cannot** imagine how many people are passing every day that place. If you come to New York, you **should** visit all the nice places here. There are a lot. But you **must** be very in time if you want to have a chance to fetch a look on the attractions.

Close to every quarter of a district there are a lot of parks. You can do a lot of things there, but not everything. You **must** not play football in front of the pick-nick places. You **should** come to one, it is really nice to have one there. You **can** skate in the skater corners, but there are many bad guys, so you **should** not do that. You **can** also ride the bicycle, but you **must not** that on the greensides.

Test 103 – Verben mit Adverbien und Präpositionen

15 Punkte

		up	out	down	on	off	along	through	away	over
a)	look	☒	☒	☒				☒		☒
b)	turn	☒	☒	☒	☒	☒				
c)	take		☒		☒	☒			☒	☒
d)	go	☒	☒	☒	☒			☒	☒	☒
e)	hang	☒	☒		☒					
f)	pick	☒								
g)	tidy	☒								
h)	fall		☒	☒				☒		
i)	break	☒	☒	☒						
j)	sit				☒	☒				
k)	blow	☒	☒							
l)	get	☒	☒		☒	☒	☒	☒	☒	☒
m)	carry			☒	☒					
n)	set	☒				☒				
o)	write			☒	☒					

Test 104 – Verben mit Adverbien und Präpositionen

10 Punkte

a) on   e) along   i) off
b) down   f) up   j) after
c) up   g) through
d) for   h) at

10 Punkte

a) broke up   f) get going
b) keep in touch   g) get away
c) passed away   h) stand up
d) look forward to   i) going down
e) carry on   j) throw off

Test 105 – Verben mit Adverbien und Präpositionen

5 Punkte

a) on
b) after
c) at
d) off
e) on

9 Punkte

a) up   d) in   g) out
b) up   e) out   h) off
c) back   f) up   i) on

Test 106 – Verben mit zwei Objekten

4 Punkte

a) **1)** SVOO – subject, verb, object, object

b) **1)** Sachobjekt und Personenobjekt
 3) direktes Objekt und indirektes Objekt.

c) **2)** Das Objekt mit der wichtigsten Information steht immer am Satzende.

A2 9 Punkte

a) Jenny has bought lots of Christmas presents for her friends.

b) She has brought the presents to their Christmas dinner.

c) She has bought Lisa a new pullover.

d) She has bought a new book for Ben.

e) She has bought Tim a new game.

f) Hey Lisa, can you show me your new pullover?

g) Ben, could you read the new book to me?

h) Tim, can you play your new game with me?

i) Lisa, Ben, and Tim give Jenny a lot of hugs.

Test 107 – Verben mit zwei Objekten

A1 18 Punkte

a) to bring

b) /

c) to cook

d) to name

e) to make

f) to offer

g) to read

h) /

i) to type

j) /

k) /

l) to ask

m) to show

n) to explain

o) to tell

p) /

q) to write

r) /

s) to lend

t) to play

u) /

v) to tell

w) to translate

x) to give

y) /

z) to send

A2 7 Punkte

a) Jenny bought a new stuffed animal for her little brother.

b) Sarah told the secret to her best friend.

c) Sarah promised Ben to keep his secret.

d) Hannah sent a birthday card to her grandma.

e) Charlotte typed Ben a love message.

f) The friendly shop assistant sold Jenny the stuffed animal.

g) The shop assistant offered Jenny a good price.

Test 108 – Verben mit zwei Objekten

A1 5 Punkte

a) Lisa writes a Christmas card to her grandma every year.

b) The shop assistant never offers good prices for footballs to clients.

c) Ben gave his girlfriend a kiss for the first time yesterday.

d) Every evening, the mother reads a chapter of the book to her children.

e) Grandma Rose explained the recipe to her grandchildren yesterday

A2 5 Punkte

a) Sarah was told a secret by Dan.

b) I was shown how to cook Lasagna by my mum.

c) I received a picture of my cousin's trip to Spain yesterday.

d) We bought a Christmas tree from the friendly man this morning.

e) I was asked about the party by my sister.

Test 109 – Verben als Substantive

A1 3 Punkte

a) **2)** Um ein doppeltes Substantiv wegzulassen. So hört sich der Satz besser an und man vermeidet Wiederholungen.

b) **1)** Ein substantiviertes Adjektiv wird immer klein geschrieben.

c) **2)** Wenn ein Adjektiv substantiviert wird, steht es immer für mehrere Personen oder Dinge.

A2 5 Punkte

a) /

b) The rich smoke less than the poor.

c) The younger do more sports than the older.

d) /

e) /

Test 110 – Verben als Substantive

A1 4 Punkte

a) **3)** Adjektive können in der Grundform und in der ersten und zweiten Steigerungsform substantiviert werden.
5) Adjektive können im Positiv, Komparativ und Superlativ substantiviert werden.

b) **3)** Substantivierte Adjektive stehen immer ohne Pluralendung.
4) Da substantiverte Adjektive immer für Gruppen von Dingen oder Personen stehen, steht auch das Verb des Satzes immer in der Pluralform.

A2 3 Punkte

a) young – younger – the youngest

b) healthy – healthier – the healthiest

c) bad – worse – the worst

A3 3 Punkte

a) The young have less job experience than the old.

b) The healthiest live the longest.

c) The worse are more effective for your body. (context of sports exercises)

Test 111 – Verben als Substantive

A1 3 Punkte

a) My sister always tries to see the best in people.

b) The healthiest food is often more expensive.

c) The older people often can't live on the fifth floor, if the house doesn't have an elevator.

A2 3 Punkte

a)

b) The educated often earn more.

c)

A3 3 Punkte

a) The young should help the old.

b) Are the tall/small more beautiful than the small/tall?

c) The friendly are often more successful.

Test 112 – Abschlusstest

A1 **4 Punkte**

a) On Sundays I take out my dog to play.

b) Does it rain in England every day?

c) They don't like to ride their old bikes.

d) We are not driving to the city right now.

A2 **6 Punkte**

a) doesn't play – wins

b) don't watch – am doing

c) likes – want

d) listening – playing

e) read – reads

f) don't go – are being

A3 **6 Punkte**

a) was playing – arrived

b) became – was travelling

c) did – go

d) were – waiting – came

e) said – wasn't feeling – talked

f) were – doing – heard

A4 **6 Punkte**

a) have not/haven't forgotten

b) Has – been

c) has repaired

d) Have – searched

e) have bought

f) has – gone

A5 **6 Punkte**

a) will spend

b) are going to stay

c) will light up

d) will tell

e) are going to miss

f) is going to throw

A6 **6 Punkte**

a) Can I go to the cinema, please?

b) She told them she might stay at home, but wasn't sure.

c) He needn't take the car. It isn't that far.

d) She walks to school every day.

e) Open the window.

f) I can't swim. I've never learned it.

A7 **7 Punkte**

a) go – was having

b) makes – ate – was working

c) came – was being

d) do – want – take

e) Have got

f) Have got

A8 **6 Punkte**

a) my/our – he

b) I – my – our – we

c) they – them

d) I – your – you – me

e) my – you – it

f) their – ours

✂

Bitte hier ausfüllen

und in der nächstgelegenen Schülerhilfe vor Ort abgeben.
Weitere Infos über die Schülerhilfe unter www.schuelerhilfe.de.

Vorname   Name

PLZ   Ort

Straße   Geburtsdatum

Telefon   E-Mail